FAITH OF OUR FATHERS

AN AMERICAN CATHOLIC HISTORY

by

Edward F. Mannino

WingSpan Press

Printed in the United States of America
Published by WingSpan Press, Livermore, CA
www.wingspanpress.com
The WingSpan name, logo and colophon
are the trademarks of WingSpan Publishing.

First Edition 2012

Publisher's Cataloging-in-Publication Data

Mannino, Edward F.
Faith of our fathers : an American catholic history / by
Edward F. Mannino.
p. cm.
ISBN 978-1-59594-477-1 (pbk.)
ISBN 978-1-59594-688-1 (hardcover)
ISBN 978-1-59594-790-1 (ebk.)
1. Catholic Church—United States—History. 2. Catholic
Church—United States—Influence.   I. Title.
BX1406.3 .M365 2012
282—dc23

                                    2012942236

For my Grandson, Henry Mannino

"Faith of our fathers, we will strive
To win all nations unto thee,
And through the truth that comes from God,
Mankind shall then be truly free."

Frederick W. Faber

CONTENTS

ACKNOWLEDGEMENTS

The idea for this book originated in a seminar on The American Catholic Experience which I taught in the College of General Studies of the University of Pennsylvania in 2006. My students included men and women of several different faiths, including Catholics, Baptists, a Mormon and a Muslim. Their intelligent inquiries and engaged discussion of the topics covered in that seminar encouraged me to write this book. I acknowledge their contributions and extend my thanks to each of them.

The Prologue is a significantly expanded version of a lecture on "The Role of Catholicism and the Catholic Conscience in American History" which I presented at the Cathedral of the Immaculate Conception in Camden, New Jersey, on November 9, 2006, as part of its Cathedral Forum Series. My thanks are owed to Reverend Monsignor Michael T. Mannion, S.T.L. for the invitation to present on this topic, and for his gracious support for it.

Chapters 1, 2, and 4 include much expanded versions of presentations on Flannery O'Connor, Thomas Merton, and Bruce Springsteen which I gave on October 13, 2010, at Saint Rose of Lima Church in North Wales, Pennsylvania, on "Catholics in the Arts and Media." I owe a considerable debt of gratitude to Reverend Monsignor Daniel A. Murray, S.T.L., S.S.L., for his invitation to present a series of talks at Saint Rose, and for his enthusiastic support for that series.

Finally, to my wife, Toni O'Connell, who read the entire manuscript, as well as several of its prior incarnations, I express my love for the joy and wisdom she has brought to my life.

CHRONOLOGY

1774   Elizabeth Seton born
1776   American Catholic population: 25,000*
1789   American Catholic population: 30,000
1805   Elizabeth Seton converts to Catholicism
1820   American Catholic population: 195,000
1821   Elizabeth Seton dies
1826   American Catholic population: 250,000
1830   American Catholic population: 318,000
1834   Gaston opinion in *State v. Will* reversing murder conviction of slave who killed overseer
        Burning of Ursuline Convent in Charlestown, Massachusetts
1835   North Carolina Constitutional Convention changes provision limiting officeholders to Protestants
1836   *Maria Monk's Awful Disclosures* published
1838   Gaston opinion in *State v. Manuel* on citizenship for freed blacks
1840   American Catholic population: 663,000
1844   Philadelphia Bible Riots
1850   American Catholic population: 1,088,000 to 1,606,000
1851   Rose Hawthorne born
1857   *Dred Scott v. Sandford* declares Missouri Compromise unconstitutional and holds slavery protected by Fifth Amendment
1858   Katherine Drexel born
1860   American Catholic population: 3,100,000
1866   Pierce Butler born
1870   American Catholic population: 3,500,000 to 4,500,000
1873   Al Smith born
1877   Great Railroad Strike
1880   American Catholic population: 6,259,000
1886   Haymarket Square Riot in Chicago
1887   Cardinal Gibbons' letter to Vatican supporting Knights of Labor
1890   American Catholic population: 7,300,000 to 8,900,000

1891   *Rerum Novarum* encyclical of Pope Leo XIII
Rose Hawthorne converts to Catholicism
Katherine Drexel founds Blessed Sacrament Sisters

1892   Homestead Mill Strike in Pennsylvania
Populist Party founded

1894   Pullman Strike

1895   Fulton Sheen born

1900   American Catholic population: 12,041,000

1902   Pennsylvania Anthracite Coal Strike

1903   Al Smith first elected to New York State Assembly

1906   Father John Ryan's *A Living Wage* published

1910   American Catholic population: 16,363,000
Rose Hawthorne founds Dominican Sisters, Congregation of St. Rose of Lima

1915   Thomas Merton born in France

1918   Al Smith elected New York Governor (reelected in 1922, 1924, and 1926)

1919   U.S. Catholic Bishops' *Program of Social Reconstruction* published

1920   American Catholic population: 18,000,000

1922   Pierce Butler named to Supreme Court
Model Eugenics Law drafted

1924   Al Smith nominated presidential candidate of Democratic Party

1925   Flannery O'Connor born
Robert Kennedy born
Katherine Drexel founds Xavier College in New Orleans for African-American students
Ku Klux Klan 500,000 March on Washington, D.C., protesting Al Smith's nomination

1926   Fulton Sheen's *God and Intelligence in Modern Philosophy* published
Rose Hawthorne dies

1927   *Buck v. Bell* upholds Virginia eugenics law on compulsory sterilization

1928   Al Smith loses presidential election to Herbert Hoover
Michael Harrington born

1930   American Catholic population: 20,000,000

1930s   Father Charles Coughlin's "Golden Hour of the Little Flower" radio program airs

1930-1952   Fulton Sheen on "The Catholic Hour" radio program

1933   Dorothy Day begins publication of *The Catholic Worker* newspaper

1936-1939   The Spanish Civil War

1937   Father John LaFarge's *Interracial Justice* published

1938   "Boys Town" movie

1939   Pierce Butler dies

1940   American Catholic population: 21,000,000
Frank Murphy named to Supreme Court
"The Fighting 69th" movie

1941   Thomas Merton enters the Trappist order in Gethsemani, Kentucky

1943-1944   *Japanese Internment Cases* decided

1944   Al Smith dies
"Going My Way" movie

1945   "The Bells of St. Mary's" movie

1948   Thomas Merton's autobiography, *The Seven Storey Mountain,* published

1949   Frank Murphy dies
Bruce Springsteen born

1952-1957   Fulton Sheen's "Life Is Worth Living" television series airs

1952   Robert Kennedy joins Senator Joseph McCarthy's Permanent Investigations Committee

1953   Flannery O'Connor's "A Good Man Is Hard To Find" published

1954   Flannery O'Connor's "A Temple of the Holy Ghost" published
"On the Waterfront" movie

1955   William Buckley begins publication of the *National Review*
Katherine Drexel dies

1956   Fulton Sheen named Archbishop of Rochester, New York
William Brennan named to Supreme Court

1959   Robert Kennedy resigns from Permanent Investigations Committee

1960   American Catholic population: 42,000,000

1961   Robert Kennedy appointed Attorney General of the United States

1962   Thomas Merton's *New Seeds of Contemplation* published
Michael Harrington's *The Other America* published

1963   Flannery O'Connor's "Revelation" published
Abington School District v. Schempp holds Bible-reading in public schools unconstitutional

1964   Flannery O'Connor dies
Robert Kennedy elected United States Senator from New York

1968   Robert Kennedy assassinated
Thomas Merton dies in Asia
Michael Harrington named chairman of the American Socialist Party

1972   William Brennan's concurring opinion in *Furman v. Georgia* on the unconstitutionality of the death penalty

1973   *Roe v. Wade* holds women possess a constitutional right to make reproductive decisions

1975   Elizabeth Seton canonized a saint
Bruce Springsteen's "Born to Run" album released

1979   Fulton Sheen dies

1980   American Catholic population: 47,502,000 to 49,812,000
Fulton Sheen's autobiography, *Treasure in Clay*, published posthumously

1982   Bruce Springsteen's "Nebraska" album released

1986   Antonin Scalia named to Supreme Court

1987   Anthony Kennedy named to Supreme Court
Edwards v. Aguillard holds Louisiana Creation Science Act unconstitutional

1989   Michael Harrington dies
Project H.O.M.E. started in Philadelphia by Mary Scullion and Joan Dawson

1990   American Catholic population: 46,000,000 to 53,385,000
William Brennan retires from Supreme Court

1991   Clarence Thomas named to Supreme Court

1995   American Catholic population: 60,190,605

2000   Katherine Drexel canonized a saint

2003   *Lawrence v. Texas* holds criminalization of voluntary gay
       sex unconstitutional
2005   John Roberts named Chief Justice of the United States
2006   Samuel Alito named to Supreme Court
2007   *Gonzales v. Carhart* upholds federal ban on partial-birth
       abortions
2008   American Catholic population: 68,000,000
       Bruce Springsteen receives Kennedy Center Lifetime
       Achievement Award
2009   Sonia Sotomayor named to Supreme Court
       Mary Scullion named one of World's Most Influential
       People by *Time* Magazine
2011   *Snyder v. Phelps* holds Westboro Baptists have
       constitutional right to picket military funeral

* There are wide variations in the various estimates of the American Catholic population over time. These estimates of the American Catholic population up to 1995 are taken from *The Encyclopedia of American Catholic History*, eds., Michael Glazier and Thomas J. Shelley (Collegeville, MN: The Liturgical Press, 1997), 288.

INTRODUCTION

This is a book about cultural history, not one about theology or ecclesiology. One of four Americans today is a professed Catholic, while one in three was born Catholic. The difference is explained by the large number of "retired" Catholics (as the actor Peter O'Toole calls them) who moved away from that faith at some point in their lives. Catholics today include the Mexican immigrant picking lettuce on a California farm, the African-American Georgetown graduate who became the head of the Republican National Committee in 2009, and the Chief Justice of the United States — along with five of his fellow justices, two of whom are Italian-Americans, one an African-American, one an Hispanic woman, and the fifth of Irish ancestry. Twenty-eight percent of the members of the House of Representatives in the 112th U.S. Congress were Catholics, split almost evenly, with 61 Republicans and 64 Democrats, while 15 of the 100 senators were Catholic. Catholics are also represented in the ranks of prominent historians and commentators, ranging from the liberal left of E. J. Dionne, Thomas Cahill, and Garry Wills to the conservative right of George Weigel and the late Richard John Neuhaus. Catholics are gay and straight; conservative and liberal; single, married and divorced; young and old; practicing and non-practicing. Like Walt Whitman, Catholics contain multitudes.

This book proceeds on the premise that these current and former Catholics share a common heritage of Catholic thought which often has penetrated to the very core of their lived values. As Bruce Springsteen has observed, "once you're a Catholic, there's no getting out."

In the Prologue of Part I, we trace how the Catholic conscience, as a largely minority voice in earlier American life, critiqued the American Republic; defended the rights of the laborer in the Gilded Age; opposed eugenics in the early twentieth century; defended and served the poor, while energizing political and economic reform, in the New Deal years; led the Cold War fight opposing Communism in the 1950s and beyond; and fought racism in American society. More recently, Catholics evolved an overall Gospel of Life, opposing abortion, euthanasia, and capital punishment as part of that effort, while Catholic authors and artists brought a Catholic message to a broader audience of Americans, both Catholic and non-Catholic.

In Part II, we examine the influence of six influential Catholics from the twentieth (and in one case the twenty-first) century. This Part begins with Flannery O'Connor, examining how her fiction emphasizes the action of grace on smug Christians who see themselves as better than others, and as already saved. Through the intervention of calamitous events, these "Christian atheists" come to see the inadequacy of their faith life and are changed. Next, we review the life and work of Thomas Merton, examining his influence on countless Americans, both Catholic and non-Catholic, for whom he served as a type of spiritual director. Merton warned his many readers of the spiritual dangers of wearing the mask of a false self, and counseled them to practice contemplation in their daily lives. While living the life of a Trappist priest, Merton also became a social activist through his writings, which protested war, nuclear weapons, and racism. Our third subject in this Part is Bishop Fulton J. Sheen, who became the first Catholic televangelist. We review his remarkable career, focusing on his hit television series, "Life Is Worth Living," which, at its peak, reached 30 million viewers. Sheen brought his Thomistic message that "faith depends upon reason" to his viewers in simple, understandable talks which were unscripted. Fourth, we look at Bruce Springsteen, whose songs incorporate Catholic themes and symbols, and encapsulate his lifelong search for faith and meaning. Springsteen acknowledges his debt to Flannery O'Connor in his songwriting, noting that her fiction encouraged him to compose his own stories, in the form of songs, setting forth a map for his listeners to follow to deal with the complexities of their daily lives. Finally, the religiously-themed poetry of Denise Levertov and John Berryman is examined against the contexts of their very different lives.

The third Part of this book focuses upon three Catholics from American public life, including Al Smith, who was the first of the three Catholics who ran for president of the United States as the candidate of the Democratic Party, and Robert F. Kennedy, who served as Attorney General of the United States and a United States senator representing the state of New York, before his tragic assassination in 1968, during his presidential campaign. The third individual whose life and works are examined in this Part is Michael Harrington. Although born Catholic and educated in Catholic schools through college, Harrington lost his faith. While mainly forgotten today, he wrote the enormously influential book, *The Other America*, in 1962. The book examined the plight of the poor in the United States and was a major influence on President Lyndon B. Johnson in his "War on Poverty." Harrington's work relied heavily upon the influences of his Catholic education and background.

The fourth Part of this book examines the influence of their religion on Catholic judges. We trace how the core Catholic concept of human dignity has variously and selectively been utilized by Catholic judges, both conservative and liberal, in explaining the reasoning of their decisions in their opinions. To do this, we review decisions opposing the mistreatment of slaves by the early nineteenth century state supreme court justice, William Gaston of North Carolina, and then turn to decisions by several Catholic justices who served on the Supreme Court of the United States in the twentieth and twenty-first centuries. We look first at the work of Pierce Butler in the area of the rights of the criminal defendant, and then examine Frank Murphy's opinions regarding the constitutionality of detaining Japanese-Americans during World War II. We also review William Brennan's decisions on capital punishment, as well as Anthony Kennedy's opinions on issues involving human dignity, including abortion, gay sexual relations, and the death penalty.

The fifth Part of this book examines how American nuns have helped the helpless of American society through their ministries. We review the work of four nuns, including two canonized saints, Elizabeth Ann Bayley Seton and Katherine Drexel. Seton converted from the Episcopal religion after her husband's death and started the first American parochial school for poor girls, going on to found a religious order. Mother Katherine Drexel was a member of the wealthy Philadelphia investment banking family, but left a life of luxury to found an order of nuns who ministered to Native Americans and African-Americans. She used her inheritance to start schools for Native Americans and blacks, including Xavier University in New

Orleans, the first Catholic college for African-Americans. We also review the life of Mother Rose Hawthorne, named a Servant of God, but not yet canonized as a saint. Like Elizabeth Seton, Hawthorne was a married woman, a mother, and a convert. Her father was the famous American writer Nathaniel Hawthorne. Rose Hawthorne also founded an order of sisters, devoted to the care of terminally ill, poor victims of cancer, for whom the order provides free medical care. The final woman religious is Sister Mary Scullion, a twenty-first century advocate for the homeless. Sister Mary founded Project H.O.M.E., which continues to provide housing, education, and employment to the homeless of Philadelphia.

In the Conclusion, we trace how Americans' perception of Catholics has changed from the rabid "anti-popery" "Whore of Babylon" view documented in the Prologue to a sympathetic view of Catholics as part of the American mainstream. We do this through the lens of popular culture, looking at movies and television shows which portray Catholic lay people and religious as a vital part of the American tapestry.

PART I

PROLOGUE

PROLOGUE

THE CATHOLIC CONSCIENCE IN AMERICAN HISTORY

"Should the present schemes of arbitrary power succeed, the Scarlet Whore would soon get mounted on her horned Beast in America, and, with the CUP OF ABOMINATION in her hand, ride triumphant over the heads of true Protestants, making multitudes DRUNK WITH THE WINE OF HER FORNICATIONS."

From a sermon by Henry Cumings (1776)

Minister Cumings was protesting the Quebec Act of 1774, in which England had permitted Canadian Catholics to practice their religion openly in that country. He and many New Englanders had long opposed "popery" as inconsistent with democracy, and even distrusted the mother country, with its Church of England. They feared that England would establish that church as the official religion in the American colonies, or worse yet, turn to Catholicism. Catholics were despised and distrusted, and their religion was identified with the great Beast or "Scarlet Whore" of the Book of Revelation, dating back to the Puritan exodus from England to build "a city on a hill" in the new land of America. This distrust of Catholics was only exacerbated by the experience of the Seven Years, or "French and Indian," War, which ended in 1763. During that war, the French Catholics, aided and abetted by their pagan Indian allies, tormented American settlers, often with gruesome barbarities. Moreover, during the reigns of Charles II and James II, who were allied with the Catholic cause in England, some New England colonies lost their royal charters. The Quebec Act broke open once again the festering sore of anti-popery in America, continuing an antipathy toward all things Catholic which lasted for over two centuries in the new country. It was not until after World War II that Catholics at last began to be accepted fully as Americans in what was still a predominately Protestant country and culture. Distrust and suspicion, often morphing into actual hostility, marred the relationships between Catholic and Protestant in America from the eighteenth to the early twentieth century.

A graphic example of such hostility occurred in 1844, in Philadelphia, the birthplace of American freedom. On July 4, 1844, some 70,000 people marched against the Catholic population of that city, as part of a two-month period of rioting which became known as the "Bible Riots" of 1844. At issue was the compulsory reading in the Philadelphia public schools of the King James (Protestant) version of both religions'sacred scriptures. In both May and July, Catholic residences and businesses were torched, Catholics and Protestants shot and killed one another, and St. Michael's Catholic Church, St. Augustine's Catholic Church, St. Philip Neri's Catholic Church, and a Sisters of Charity seminary were set on fire by Protestant mobs, who stopped a fire company from combating the fire at St. Michael's. Similar riots over the use of the Protestant Bible in the public schools broke out during the same period in New York and St. Louis. The controversy was incendiary, both literally and politically, and had a long life. Indeed, it would take nearly 120 years before the Catholic position in the Philadelphia Bible Riots was vindicated by the Supreme Court of the United States in *Abington School District v. Schempp* (1963), which ruled that all compulsory reading of the Bible in public schools was unconstitutional under the First Amendment's Establishment Clause.

While the burning of Catholic churches and convents was rare, the Philadelphia Bible Riots were not the only venue in which they occurred. Perhaps the most notorious example happened on August 11, 1834, in Charlestown, Massachusetts, near Boston, when the Ursuline Sisters' convent was burned by a mob of Protestant workingmen who had been inflamed by Protestant preachers' attacks on Catholicism. Lyman Beecher, a noted evangelical of the day, had delivered a sermon the night before the attack assailing the Ursulines, under the title "The Devil and the Pope of Rome," and other Protestant clergy joined in the condemnation of Catholicism from their pulpits. At the time, a nun had left the convent and was rumored to have been kidnapped by other nuns and forcibly taken back. This conjured up the familiar stereotype of the times of convents as places of captivity for young girls who became the sex slaves of a lustful Catholic priesthood. Indeed, the best-selling book in the United States before *Uncle Tom's Cabin* (1852) was the scandalous *Maria Monk's Awful Disclosures of the Hotel Dieu Nunnery in Montreal* (1836), which sold over 300,000 copies before the Civil War. It purported to record horrible atrocities performed on women by priests in convents, including the smothering of their newborn babies (after they were baptized, of course) who had been fathered by priests through the rape of innocent postulants.

In the Boston of 1834 and the Philadelphia of 1844, Catholics were thus distrusted and viewed as un-American not only for protesting Bible reading, which was seen as part of the American civic religion of the nineteenth century, but also for being mindless followers of a foreign potentate in Rome. This negative view of Catholics as bad Americans predated even the American Founders, and extended well into the twentieth century. For example, a young Alexander Hamilton protested the Quebec Act of 1774 on the grounds that it set up an "arbitrary power, and its great engine the Popish religion," in Canada, while John Jay, later the first Chief Justice of the United States, saw that Act as permitting the toleration of "a religion fraught with sanguinary and impious tenets," which had "deluged [England] in blood, and dispersed bigotry, persecution, murder and rebellion through every part of the world." In a similar vein, Patriot leader Sam Adams of Massachusetts warned his followers in 1768 that "What we have above everything else to fear is POPERY."

This engrained anti-Catholicism continued well after adoption of the Constitution. In an 1821 letter from former president John Adams to his old opponent, former president Thomas Jefferson, for example, the two found one thing they could agree on, when Adams asked rhetorically (in his view) whether " a free Government [can] possibly exist with a Roman Catholic Religion?"

This view continued unabated after the Founding Generation. Reflecting the immigration of over two million Irish to the United States in the period from 1840 through 1860, some new political parties made anti-Catholicism a prime portion of their political platforms. The most notorious was the American Party, popularly called the "Know Nothings." Founded in 1850, the party had one million members by 1854, elected governors in eight states and mayors in Boston, Chicago and Philadelphia. With such a power base, the American Party became a leading contender for the presidency in 1856. Its unsuccessful candidate that year was former president Millard Fillmore, who captured over 870,000 votes -nearly 22 percent of the popular vote in that election. The American Party opposed foreigners, particularly Catholics, and in states like Massachusetts took control of the legislature, mandating use of the King James Bible in public schools and banning Catholics from being hired on public sector jobs. In the same period, the Free Soil Party, which later merged into the new Republican Party, extolled the virtues of a Protestant America. One adherent announced that he stood for "freedom, temperance and Protestantism, against slavery, rum and Romanism." The Whig Party of Henry Clay and Daniel Webster (and the young Abraham Lincoln) also showed hostility to Catholics, the vast majority of whom were members of the rival Democratic Party of Andrew Jackson and his successors. Lincoln himself stood against anti-Catholicism, attacking the American Party's prejudices. Lincoln stated that "as a nation, we began by declaring that *all men are created equal*... When the Know Nothings get control, it will read 'All men are created equal' except negroes, *and foreigners, and catholics.*"

Anti-Catholicism did not end with slavery after the Civil War. Ralph Waldo Emerson saw fit to proclaim in 1863, the midpoint of that war, that "the political character of the Roman Church...makes it incompatible with our institutions, & unwelcome here." And Elizabeth Cady Stanton, a fierce proponent of women's suffrage, proclaimed in 1869 that if the Catholic idea of authority "finds lodgment in the minds of this people, we ring the death-knell of American liberties."

The Republican presidents of the 1870s and 1880s sounded similar alarms against Catholicism. In 1875, President Ulysses S. Grant opposed any financial aid to "sectarian" schools, wanted to tax church property, and foresaw a future where "patriotism and intelligence" might contend with "superstition, ambition and ignorance." Grant called for education as a remedy to protect Americans from "sink[ing] into acquiescence to the will of intelligence, whether directed by the *demagogue* or by *priestcraft.*"

While campaigning for governor of Ohio, future president Rutherford B. Hayes attacked his Democratic opponents for permitting Catholic priests to visit prisoners and those in asylums. In the same vein, another future president, James A. Garfield, warned of Catholics as a threat to "modern civilization," and saw Democratic gains in 1876 as rooted in the "combined power of rebellion, Catholicism and whiskey."

Protestant leaders were openly and outspokenly opposed to Catholicism. James G. Blaine, a Republican, proposed a constitutional amendment banning any financial aid to parochial schools. In the 1876 Senate Debates on the Blaine Amendment, the Catholic Church was described as "the most powerful religious sect that the world has ever known, or probably ever will know — a church that is universal, ubiquitous, aggressive, restless, and untiring," while the Pope was targeted as "the old Pope of Rome,... the great bull that we are all to attack." Blaine lost his presidential bid in 1884 to the Democrat Grover Cleveland partially because a Protestant minister supporting Blaine attacked the Democratic Party of Cleveland as the party of "rum, Romanism and rebellion."

By the late 1880s, a new group, the American Protective Association, emerged as a leading force against Catholics. Its members all were required to take certain oaths, the fourth of which had provisions which mandated the member to "solemnly promise and swear" that he or she "will use my utmost power to strike the shackles and chains of blind obedience to the Roman Catholic Church from the hampered and bound consciences of a priest-ridden and church-oppressed people," as well as to "use my influence to promote the interest of all Protestants everywhere in the world that I may be," and to further swear that "I will not employ a Roman Catholic in any capacity if I can procure the services of a Protestant."

Even Walter Rauschenbusch, the well-known liberal minister of the Social Gospel, wrote in his 1907 book, *Christianity and the Social Crisis*, that "The Catholic Church by its organization tends to keep alive and active the despotic spirit of decadent Roman civilization in which it originated," and "The Roman Church crumbles away before [Protestantism] in our country and can only save its adherents by quarantining its children in parochial schools and its men and women in separate social and benevolent societies."

These few examples show that Catholics, from before the founding of the nation through the late nineteenth century and well into the twentieth, were continually marginalized by the leaders of

American politics and society. As such, Catholics were not part of the dominant culture and were consequently freed to call for reform as social critics of American excess. In this Prologue, we will examine six examples of such critical Catholic commentary on American economic and social issues, starting with the mid nineteenth century.

ORESTES BROWNSON CRITIQUES THE AMERICAN REPUBLIC

Orestes Brownson was the most important lay Catholic intellectual in the United States in the nineteenth century. The English Catholic Cardinal, John Henry Newman, called Brownson "by far the greatest thinker America has ever produced."

Brownson travelled a long and tortuous path to Catholicism. He was born in Vermont in 1803, and raised in the Congregationalist religion. Over the years, he switched religions frequently. In 1822, he became a Presbyterian, but switched denominations to become a Universalist in 1826. By 1832, he had switched again, this time becoming a Unitarian minister in 1832. At that point in his life, he opposed organized religion, and saw the priesthood as despotic. Brownson was then a Jacksonian Democrat, with a strong interest and participation in the Transcendentalist Movement of the time.

All this changed in 1844, when Brownson became a Roman Catholic, which he remained until his death thirty two years later. His conversion was sparked by personal study with the assistance of a priest, and by his conviction that society was a collective whole. He came to oppose the individualism of the times, which he traced to the influence of the Protestant religions in America.

In 1844, at the time of his conversion, Brownson began publication of *Brownson's Quarterly Review*, which continued until 1864, and resumed publication from 1873 to 1875. This journal gave Brownson a pulpit from which he proclaimed on a myriad of subjects from his liberal Catholic perspective, which ran ahead of the Vatican approach to social issues. He opposed slavery before the Roman Catholic Church did. He also opposed the system of American Catholic schools, which he saw as a barrier to Catholic integration into the broader society, and spoke out in favor of social reforms before Pope Leo XIII did years later.

Brownson saw the Catholic religion as the only one which could make American democracy work, by imposing restraint upon the rampant individualism he witnessed in the mid nineteenth century American society. He criticized the compact theory of government, and saw Americans as a single people, observing that "The people taken collectively are society, and society is a living organism, not a mere aggregation of individuals."

Catholics were seen by Brownson as an increasing force in American society – "an integral, living, and growing element in the American population, quite too numerous, too wealthy, and too influential to be ignored." Indeed, his triumphalism led him to conclude that "Catholics are better fitted by their religion to comprehend the real character of the American constitution than any other class of Americans" because, among other attributes, "their church everywhere opposes the socialistic movements of the age, all movements in behalf of barbarism, and they may always be counted on to resist the advance of socialistic democracy."

While Brownson was only a minor figure intellectually in the Protestant society of the nineteenth century, he has become a conservative icon in the twentieth and twenty first centuries. This is attributable to his increasingly conservative views rooted in a natural rights philosophy which emphasized the need for a collaborative commonwealth. His views on the dangers to such a society prospering in his America are set forth at length in his book, *The American Republic: Its Constitution, Tendencies, and Destiny*, which he published in 1865, as the Civil War ended.

The American Republic treats at length with many issues, ranging from general philosophical discussions of the nature of society and sovereignty and the differences between written and "providential" constitutions of a nation, to specific analyses of American slavery, secession of the southern states, and the probable nature of post Civil war reconstruction. For our purposes, his most interesting comments relate to his view that "The United States, or the American Republic, has a mission, and is chosen of God for the realization of a great idea." That idea "is liberty, indeed, but *liberty with law, and law with liberty.* Yet its mission is not so much the realization of liberty as the realization of the true idea of the state, which secures at once the authority of the public and the freedom of the individual – *the sovereignty of the people without social despotism, and individual freedom without anarchy."*

To secure its mission, Brownson warned his fellow Americans about the need to oppose two approaches which were then common in his American society. These were individualism, on the one hand, and what he called "humanitarianism, socialism, or centralized democracy," on the other hand. He saw individual liberty as strong in the South and a by-product of Jeffersonian democracy; in this form, it is "pure individualism—philosophically considered, pure egoism, which says, 'I am God.'" Such a concept "may be abused, and so explained as to deny the rights of society."

Conversely, "no political system that runs to the opposite extreme, and absorbs the individual in the state, stands the least chance of any general or permanent success till Christianity is extinguished." Brownson took aim at the Northern abolitionists as following this approach, accusing them of seeing "humanity, superior to individuals, superior to states, governments, and laws, and holds that he may trample on them all or give them to the winds at the call of humanity or 'the higher law.'" This approach "is as indefensible as the personal or egoistical democracy of the slaveholders and their sympathizers," and "pure socialism is as incompatible with American democracy as pure individualism."

Brownson summed up his warning to America regarding the need to tame the tendencies in his society to the twin threats of individualism and humanitarianism as follows:

> "Of the several tendencies mentioned, the humanitarian tendency, egoistical at the South, detaching the individual from the race, and socialistic at the North, absorbing the individual in the race, is the most dangerous. The egoistical form is checked, sufficiently weakened by the defeat of the rebels; but the social form believes that it has triumphed, and that individuals are effaced in society, and the States in the Union. Against this, more especially should public opinion and American statesmanship be now directed...."

DEFENSE OF THE LABORER IN THE GILDED AGE

Brownson's fears about the dangers of "humanitarianism" were premature as the nineteenth century ended, but his warnings about individualism were right on point. The rise of industrial capitalism in the United States in the last half of the nineteenth century submerged any tendency towards humanitarianism in favor of an unbridled individualism manifested by the robber barons of the period.

The emergence of industrial capitalism fueled the growth of an unskilled laboring class, especially in the northern and mid-western states. Many of these workers were immigrants, and many of the immigrants in turn were Catholic. Depressions and other economic dislocations, including the Panics of 1873 and 1893, resulted in severe wage cuts between ten and forty percent being imposed unilaterally by business owners, placing already low-paid workers further into deep poverty. As a result, union membership grew and strikes became commonplace. In the early 1880s, there were on average 500 strikes annually in the United States. A decade later, the average shot up to 1300. And many of the strikes were accompanied by violence, as well as by destruction of property.

There were four great strikes in this period. The Great Railroad Strike of 1877, sparked by a ten percent wage cut, spread coast to coast, and involved the destruction of millions of dollars of railroad equipment. In 1886, as an outgrowth of a strike at McCormick Harvester, protesters and police were killed in Chicago in what became known as the Haymarket Square Riot. Andrew Carnegie's Homestead Steel Mill in Pennsylvania was the next major target in 1892, with private Pinkerton police and then the state militia battling with the Homestead steel workers, resulting in deaths on both sides. Finally, the Pullman Strike of 1894 was a response to wage cuts ranging between twenty-five and forty percent. Again, troops were called in, this time federal troops activated by the Democratic president, Grover Cleveland, with the union leader Eugene Debs being jailed for his participation in the strike. Debs became radicalized by the experience and ran for president as a socialist in each election between 1900 and 1920, except for 1916. In 1912, he received six percent of the votes cast nationally in that election, which saw Woodrow Wilson defeating President William Howard Taft and Theodore Roosevelt, the former president, running as a third party candidate.

Speaking at a commencement ceremony at the University of Iowa in 1888, Justice Samuel Freeman Miller of the Supreme Court of the United States summarized the American social situation at the time:

> "the palaces of the rich are surrounded by the hovels of the poor; the glaring lights of gas and electric lamps illuminating for the wealthy their hours of hilarity and festivity shine down upon the tenements of the lowly and the poverty stricken, and while the more favored few have all that is best in life in the way of pleasure and enjoyment, another much larger class of beings a few hundred yards away, or across the street, may be languishing in misery, burdened by poverty, and tortured by disease for which they have not the means to provide the remedy...."
>
> Miller felt the need for "the introduction of such real and genuine reforms in the fabric of social life as shall tend to ameliorate the hardships of want and to prevent all needless suffering."

By 1892, these dislocations in the social fabric generated the new Peoples (Populist) Party, with a lengthy agenda for reform. In 1896, this new party fused with the Democratic Party, putting forth the young William Jennings Bryan of Nebraska as their joint presidential candidate. Bryan attacked industry and memorably roused his followers by declaring that they shall not be "crucified upon a cross of gold." He was referring to the Republican platform commitment to a "sound money" gold standard.

But Bryan lost to William McKinley both in 1896 and 1900. The majority of the American people, considering the labor violence described above, saw labor as radical, and rejected the call for deep reform. Moreover, after Justice Miller's death in 1890, the Supreme Court strengthened the already powerful hand of business against labor by its hostility to unions under the banner of "freedom of contract." Business' attitude to unions was summarized by George F. Baer, the president of the Philadelphia and Reading Railroad. Speaking against the Pennsylvania Anthracite Coal Strike of 1902, Baer opined that "the rights and interests of the laboring man will be protected and cared for, not by the *labor agitators*, but by the *Christian men to whom God in His infinite wisdom, has given control of the property interests of the country."

In this era of Social Darwinism and freedom of contract, few spoke for the worker. Many Protestant clergy opposed unions. For example, even while denouncing the "oppressive rich," Russell Conwell, the Baptist minister who founded Temple University in Philadelphia, felt that unions were unhelpful because they forced the adoption of a uniform wage, thereby penalizing skilled laborers.

Two of those who spoke for the worker were Cardinal James Gibbons of Baltimore, and Archbishop John Ireland of St. Paul, Minnesota. Initially, their position was not popular with some of their colleagues, or with the Vatican. At the time, the Vatican was hostile to the Knights of Labor, which was an early labor union patterned on the medieval guild, and was considering condemning the American Knights of Labor, as it had earlier condemned the Canadian branch of the Knights. Gibbons, the leader of the Catholic Church in the United States, was a staunch defender of the working man. He often said that "I would rather grasp the soiled hand of the honest artisan, than touch the soft, kid-gloved hand of the dandy." He saw Christ as a "humble child of toil...the reputed son of an artisan [whose] early manhood is spent in a mechanic's shop."

Gibbons argued forcefully to the Vatican on behalf of the Knights in 1887, proclaiming that "it is evidently of supreme importance that the Church should always be found on the side of humanity, of justice toward the multitudes who compose the body of the human family." Supported by Archbishop Ireland, Gibbons attacked American monopolists for their "heartless avarice which, through greed of gain, pitilessly grinds not only the men, but particularly the women and children in various employments." Gibbons concluded that the Knights should not be condemned because of labor violence or their secrecy, but should be recognized as possessing the "right of the laboring classes to protect themselves." Indeed, in Gibbons' view, there was a corresponding "duty of the whole people to aid [the laborer] in finding a remedy against the dangers with which both civilization and the social order are menaced by avarice, oppression and corruption" because "there exist among us...grave and threatening social evils, public injustices, which call for strong resistance and legal remedy."

Gibbons and Ireland prevailed on this issue, and Pope Leo XIII advocated protection of the worker a few years later in his classic encyclical, *Rerum Novarum* (1891). There, Pope Leo called for payment of a just wage, support of collective bargaining, and provision of decent working conditions. The Vatican has continued this pro-worker advocacy for a hundred years in a number of later encyclicals, including two issued by Pope John Paul II, the first in 1971 and the second in 1991.

OPPOSITION TO EUGENICS

A third example of Catholic opposition to the prevailing American thinking is found in the Eugenics Movement of the 1920s. At that time, a new social threat arose, where the American Catholic Church was a solitary voice in favor of disadvantaged and marginalized members of American society.

The Eugenics Movement attempted to build upon the intellectual framework of the Progressive Movement of the early twentieth century in America. Viewed properly by many historians as a revolt of the Protestant elite against the emerging power of immigrants and Catholics in urban politics, the Progressive Movement supported legislation, principally at the state and local level, to impose structure and order on American society. It supported such approaches as prohibition of alcohol, Sunday closing laws, segregation of the races, prohibition of "white slave" traffic, and compulsory public education, all with a view to ordering American society and controlling the perceived threat from an immigrant and African-American population which was seen as endangering that social order.

A critical part of this ordering of society among many intellectuals and some Protestant clergy in the 1920s was the Eugenics Movement, which took its name from the Greek word for "well born." Eugenics can be viewed as the social equivalent of the General Electric management philosophy of culling its workforce to eliminate the lowest performing ten percent of employees each year. In order to eliminate the "most worthless ten percent," eugenics called for compulsory sterilization of the "unfit," including mentally and physically disabled individuals, the blind and near blind, the deaf and near deaf, and even so-called "ne'er do wells," such as the homeless, tramps, and paupers. Eugenics laws calling for compulsory sterilization were enacted in some thirty states, but were enforced methodically in only two - California and Virginia. Over 20,000 Americans were sterilized under these laws, 10,000 in California and 4,000 in Virginia. Virginia's law lasted into the 1970s. Hundreds of colleges and universities offered courses in eugenics, with an estimated attendance of some 20,000 students in 1928. The leaders of Ivy League universities on the East Coast and institutions such as Stanford University and the University of Southern California on the West Coast embraced eugenics. Adolf Hitler modeled the sterilization laws of the Third Reich on the American Model Act devised in 1922 by Harry Laughlin, an American. In Nazi Germany, 375,000 individuals were sterilized under this law.

Even after the Nazi experience turned Americans against compulsory sterilization laws, many American intellectuals continued to favor sterilization of those they believed to be undesirable, now encouraging voluntary choice. One notable proponent of voluntary sterilization was William R. Shockley, a Noble Prize winner in Physics from California who invented the transistor. Shockley advocated that some people who had below normal IQs be compensated if they chose to be sterilized. He also stated in a 1974 television interview that African Americans had "intellectual and social deficits" which were "hereditary and racially genetic in origin and thus not remediable to a major degree by practical improvements in environment."

The only organized opposition to the enactment and enforcement of eugenics laws internationally and in the United States in the 1920s and 1930s came from Catholics, both lay and clerical. In England, the Catholic author and polemicist, G. K. Chesterton, wrote a 1922 book entitled *Eugenics and Other Evils*, while Pope Pius XI condemned eugenics (as well as artificial birth control) in his 1930 encyclical, *Casti Connubii.*

In the United States, Archbishop John W. Shaw of New Orleans spoke out against eugenics. Shaw called instead for state efforts to properly house and protect the poor, rejecting attempts to attain a "millennium of supermen and superwomen as perfect specimens of the human animal, bred and reared according to the latest eugenics rules." Such criticism of eugenics was unavailing at the time, and the Supreme Court of the United States, in an opinion we will discuss in a later chapter, upheld the constitutionality of Virginia's laws in

1927. The sole dissent was registered by the court's only Catholic Justice. Within two years after that ruling, twelve states enacted new sterilization laws.

CATHOLICS, THE GREAT DEPRESSION, AND THE NEW DEAL

The Great Depression of the 1930s provided another opportunity for Catholic social teachings to be applied to the economic life of the United States. What had been rejected by the American people as too radical in the days of the Knights of Labor and Cardinal Gibbons would become more acceptable when millions of people who had been employed were now out of work. In these circumstances, the communal vision of Catholic social thought attracted some political leaders, including the incoming president, Franklin Delano Roosevelt.

In his first Inaugural Address, delivered on March 4, 1933, Roosevelt employed biblical language and a communal vision to describe the roots of the Depression. He attacked the "unscrupulous money changers," who "know only the rules of a generation of self-seekers." The new president exhorted his audience to help their "fellow men," preaching that:

> "The money changers have fled from their high seats in the temple of our civilization. We may now restore that temple to the ancient truths. The measure of the restoration lies in the extent to which we apply social values more noble than mere monetary profit....

> "These dark days will be worth all they cost us if they teach us that our true destiny is not to be ministered unto but to minister to ourselves and to our fellow men."

Roosevelt's vision drew early support from the Catholic intellectual community. The Jesuit magazine *America*, in a June 1933 piece, saw the New Deal as incorporating the views that "there are rights more sacred than the right to hold property, and...the primary function of government is to exercise due control of all the agencies in society to do justice to all, and to show favor in particular to the needy."

While President Roosevelt himself recognized that Catholic social teachings contained in papal encyclicals were more radical than his own New Deal, his programs were nevertheless affected by Catholic social thought, principally through the action of two notable Catholic priests.

The first of these was Father Charles Coughlin, the "radio priest" of the times. During the Depression, Coughlin's program, "The Golden Hour of the Little Flower," named for the recently canonized St. Therese of Lisieux in France, had forty million listeners for its Sunday evening program. Coughlin received more mail than President Roosevelt, and needed 106 clerks and four secretaries to open his mail and respond to those who wrote to him. He became politically close to Roosevelt from 1932 through 1934, praising him on the air, preaching "Roosevelt or ruin," and contending that "The New Deal is Christ's Deal." Coughlin's political platform was a mixture of the papal labor encyclicals and Populism, with a visible dose of anti-Semitism stirred in. He attacked both Marxists and "predatory capitalists," called for abolition of the Federal Reserve and the gold standard, and favored nationalization of the banks and the economy. Coughlin, whose religious congregation in Michigan was heavily seeded with automotive workers, was instrumental in pushing Roosevelt to support Social Security unemployment insurance and compensation programs as well as the National Labor Relations Act, which established a federal labor board to combat unfair labor practices, compelled union recognition, and banned anti-union "yellow dog" contracts.

Coughlin broke with Roosevelt in 1935, now characterizing his message as "Roosevelt AND ruin." He opposed Roosevelt's support of a World Court, claiming that it would invade the sovereignty of the United States, and would turn the country over to the international bankers. Coughlin also stood far to the left of Roosevelt's First New Deal, and switched his allegiance to a third party which planned to run Senator Huey P. Long for president. Long was a flamboyant populist from Louisiana who advocated "soaking the rich" with higher taxes and redistributing income. But Long was assassinated in September of 1935, and the party ran a poor third in the presidential election of 1936. Coughlin became increasingly embittered and anti-Semitic, even at times praising Adolf Hitler and the philosophy of the National Socialist Party. Coughlin's growing support of international isolationism and his anti-Semitic remarks led the Vatican to silence him completely by 1942. Nevertheless, Coughlin's early support for Roosevelt was instrumental in galvanizing additional support for the first New Deal, among both Catholics and those of other religions.

A more mainstream Catholic influence on the New Deal was Monsignor John A. Ryan, who was derisively christened "Right Reverend New Dealer" by Father Coughlin. Ryan became friendly with Roosevelt and his advisers, and gave the Benedictions at Roosevelt's second and fourth inaugurals. Ryan travelled widely in non-Catholic circles, serving on the board of the American Civil Liberties Union and other organizations, and was friendly with both Justice Louis Brandeis of the Supreme Court of the United States and the noted legal scholar Roscoe Pound. Ryan was a protégé of Archbishop John Ireland, who had sent Ryan to Catholic University in 1898, nine years after it officially opened. Ryan taught theology at Catholic University from 1915 to 1940, where he influenced many Catholic scholars.

Inspired by Pope Leo XIII's *Rerum Novarum*, Ryan's thesis was published in 1906 as *A Living Wage: Its Ethical and Economic Aspects*. Its message found support among the largely Protestant Social Gospel movement and affiliated economists such as Richard Ely. In 1916, Ryan wrote *Distributive Justice: The Right and Wrong of Our Present Distribution of Wealth*. That book called for distribution of property in a widespread fashion in order to grant both dignity and independence to the ordinary worker. Ryan saw payment of a "living wage" as a fundamental right of all workers, and supported the eight-hour day, workers' rights, progressive taxation, public housing, public ownership of utilities, worker ownership of "the instruments of production," and old age, unemployment, and health insurance. In 1919, he composed what was released as the Catholic *Bishops' Program of Social Reconstruction*, which supported many of these ideas.

Ryan's published works advanced what were then radical ideas, which found favor only in the economic shambles which were the legacy of the Great Depression. Ryan realized success in the adoption of his ideas in such programs as Social Security's old age, unemployment and health insurance, and in the National Recovery Administration, which encouraged the formation of voluntary "associations of industries," a concept supported by *Quadragesimo Anno* (1931), a papal encyclical of Pope Pius XI.

While Coughlin and Ryan focused upon political and governmental solutions to the economic dislocations caused by the Great Depression, a third Catholic, Dorothy Day, took a very different approach towards implementing the teachings of Catholic social thought at that time and beyond. A former atheist who converted to Catholicism because she saw the Catholic Church as "the church of the poor," Day began the *Catholic Worker* newspaper in 1933, in order "to call [workers'] attention to the fact that the Catholic Church has a social program." Critical of scholars who spent their time reading and writing in abstractions about the problems of poverty, Day chose instead to implement "the Little Way" of St. Therese (Father Coughlin's "Little Flower"), by serving individual poor people in a direct and personal way, feeding them, changing their bandages, and giving them shelter in what were some thirty three Catholic Worker houses throughout the United States by 1936. Her work prefigured that done later by Mother Teresa among the poor in India.

Day's social program did not concentrate on the macroeconomic reforms of Monsignor Ryan or Father Coughlin because she saw the alleviation of poverty as the personal responsibility of every person. While Day accepted the fact of poverty and suffering, and saw them as ultimately redemptive, she insisted upon "decent poverty."

Day opposed Catholic assimilation into American society, calling instead for Catholics to be what is now characterized as "a sign of contradiction" to society at large. She became a peace activist, protesting nuclear testing and air raid drills in the 1950s and 1960s, and opposing the Vietnam War thereafter. Day lived into her mid-eighties, and through her public witness became what the Catholic lay journal *Commonweal* called "the most significant, interesting, and influential person in the history of American Catholicism."

COMMUNISM, THE COLD WAR, AND RACIAL SEGREGATION

Another area of controversy in which America's Catholic population represented an important opposition voice was found in its implacable opposition to Communism before the Cold War. While some Catholic concepts found support in the New Deal, as we have seen in the discussion above, the strong Catholic opposition to Communism was not among them. Indeed, some leading New Dealers, including the State Department's Alger Hiss, were Communist agents, and much of Protestant America supported the Spanish Republican side in that nation's bloody civil war of 1936 through 1939 against the Loyalists led by General Francisco Franco. Franco, who orchestrated a coup against the elected Republicans, was a fascist supported by Germany, Italy, and the Catholic Church. The Republicans, by contrast, were supported by Soviet Russia and by many liberal Americans. In this context, Communists were seen as supporters of democracy, while the Church was seen as its enemy.

This positive view of Communism, which was held by many Americans in the 1930s, began to change dramatically after the end of World War II and the beginnings of the Cold War. The changing attitude of Americans towards the Catholic Church's opposition to Communism is graphically shown in a 1950s cartoon from the Brooklyn archdiocesan newspaper, *The Tablet*. The cartoon portrays the Catholic Church in three panels as Paul Revere, warning America about Communism in 1919 (the Bolshevik Revolution), 1935 (the Spanish Civil War), and 1950 (the Cold War). In the first two panels of the cartoon, the warning is ignored. Only in 1950 is the Catholic horseman followed by figures labeled as "politicians," "radio commentators," and "military leaders," shouting in support of the Catholic rider that "the Reds are coming."

The emerging threat posed by Communism began to be recognized by the American people generally by the 1950s, and this recognition helped the Catholic minority to be accepted more readily as authentic Americans in the Cold War era. Many Catholic politicians and clergy came to be leaders in a general American crusade against what became known as "Godless Communism." These leaders included Bishop Fulton J. Sheen, whose television program, "Life is Worth Living," topped the ratings charts in the 1950s, journalist William F. Buckley, and Senator Joseph McCarthy, whose anti-Communist message was reportedly developed with the assistance of Father Edmund Walsh of Georgetown University's Foreign Service Institute. Bishop Sheen regularly attacked the Communist philosophy, and gave a famous television presentation on "The Death of Stalin," quoting passages from Shakespeare's *Julius Caesar*, only a few days before Stalin in fact did die. While McCarthy died in 1957, after he was discredited and censured by the United States Senate, Buckley's vigorous anti-Communism continued in the pages of *The National Review*, which he started in 1955. Other Catholic groups also spearheaded efforts to distinguish the United States from Soviet Russia by embracing God publicly. For example, the Catholic Knights of Columbus were instrumental in having the words "under God" added to the Pledge of Allegiance by Congress in 1954.

The Cold War also helped erode the sway of racial segregation in the United States because America was attempting to differentiate itself from "Godless Communism," and thus needed to remove the stain of racism from the fabric of American life. Catholic Church leaders in America, as well as in the Vatican, opposed racial segregation both before and during the Cold War era. This opposition went back as far as the nineteenth century, with leaders such as Archbishop John Ireland opposing both segregation and legal bans on racial intermarriage. Father John Ryan – the "Right Reverend New Dealer" we met above – spoke out against segregation, while other, more activist, bishops attempted to dismantle segregation in their dioceses.

The most significant Catholic figure speaking out against racial segregation was the Jesuit priest, Father John LaFarge. In 1937, LaFarge wrote *Interracial Justice*, a book which characterized racism as a sin. LaFarge's book was read by Pope Pius XI, who requested LaFarge to help him write an encyclical opposing both racism and anti-Semitism. That encyclical was never published, however, because LaFarge's Jesuit Superior refused to release LaFarge's draft, and Pius died in early 1939.

By the 1950s, other Catholic theologians, including John Courtney Murray, taught that segregation was morally wrong. Not all of the Catholic clergy or laymen joined this opposition to segregation. Indeed, in the southern United States, several prominent Catholic politicians were eventually excommunicated for the sin of racism.

THE GOSPEL OF LIFE

In the last half of the twentieth century, the position of Catholics in the United States changed significantly. Rather than contending with a hostile Protestant majority, Catholics found themselves uniting with other people of faith in a mutual effort to arrest a rising tide of secularism in public life. The watershed event was the Supreme Court's decision in *Roe v. Wade* (1973), which created a constitutional right for women in making reproductive decisions. Following the *Roe* decision, Catholics stood virtually alone as opponents of abortion on demand, since many of the mainline Protestant, and even some evangelical, churches supported at least some abortion rights. Soon, however, an unprecedented alliance of conservative Catholics and Protestant evangelicals formed a coalition to oppose abortion on demand. That coalition led to expanded cooperation between the Christian churches, with a lessening of the traditional tensions between Catholics and Protestants as a welcome result.

Gradually, under the leadership of the U.S. Catholic Bishops, the Catholic pro-life movement began to embrace additional causes, not all of which were accepted by the Protestant members of the anti-abortion coalition. The resulting "Gospel of Life" advanced a comprehensive pro-life position, covering a multitude of subjects beyond abortion. These positions included opposition to abortion, assisted suicide, euthanasia, capital punishment, experimentation on embryonic stem cells, use of preemptive or preventative war, and targeting of civilians in war or antiterrorist activities. Indeed, in the area of "just war" theology, Catholic social teaching came close to heeding the activist monk Thomas Merton's lament of the 1960s that he wished Catholic opposition to the use of nuclear weapons would be as strict as its opposition to the use of birth control. While some of these antiwar stands and the opposition to stem cell research were controversial even among Catholics, the Gospel of Life continued the American Catholic tradition of prophetic warning to the broader American community, presenting a logically coherent moral teaching in an increasingly secular public square.

* * *

The journey of Catholics in the United States from members of a despised minority to mainstream citizens has been a long one, with the Catholic contribution changing from the social criticism of an outsider to the engaged critique of a neighbor. As the following chapters will demonstrate, the Catholic presence in American society has supplied many diverse voices which have called America thoughout its history to recognize and implement core spiritual and material values in the broader pluralistic society.

PART II

CATHOLICS IN AMERICAN

ARTS AND LETTERS

INTRODUCTION

In this part, we review the work of six individuals from Catholic backgrounds who incorporated Catholic themes in their work for the benefit of wide audiences, including many non-Catholics. Their work brought abstract Catholic theological concepts to life in concrete, incarnational ways, through stories, televised lectures, songs, and spiritual writings, making them available to the American public at large in understandable ways. Their contributions helped pave the way for Catholics to be accepted as part of the American mainstream, reversing the anti-Catholicism that had permeated American society for two centuries.

We begin with Flannery O'Connor, whose novels and short stories show the action of grace upon self-centered individuals who see themselves as saved and as better than those around them. O'Connor shows through the drama of her stories how the sick and disabled, the African-American workers, and the other marginalized people in her southern society are, in reality, holier than the smug "Christians" who do not actually live their religion, but treat it instead as a security blanket. Through the use of sudden flashes of insights called epiphanies, the plots of O'Connor's stories bring their protagonists to an awakening through which they come to see their shallowness, and are thus called to be saved. By showing how grace works in individual lives, rather than sermonizing abstractly about it, O'Connor brings the reality of God's work in the world vividly to life, teaching the lessons of grace better than a Sunday homily. In short, she makes grace believable.

We next turn to Thomas Merton, who became a de facto spiritual director to many Americans of all faiths through his writings. Born in France, he was left an orphan by the age of sixteen, and left Cambridge University in England under a cloud, apparently having fathered a child out of wedlock. Enrolling in

Columbia University in New York, Merton came to regret his past dissolute life and converted to Catholicism. He entered the Trappist monastery in Gethsemani, Kentucky, in 1941, and spent nearly all his life there. He died tragically in 1968 by accidental electrocution at the age of 53, in Bangkok, Thailand, in the course of an Asian journey. Merton began his monastic life in search of a holy solitude, but ultimately realized that he was brother to all people, and began to write on the ways of contemplation for the individual living in the world. He also protested the evils of racism and war, and wrote in support of the civil rights and anti-war movements. His writings call us to see the beauties of the natural world and of other men and women. From his post in the monastic refuge in Kentucky, he observed the world and acted as a "fire watcher" to alert those in the world to spiritual dangers. His prophetic work continues today through publications and retreats sponsored by the International Thomas Merton Society and the Merton Institute for Contemplative Living.

The third individual we discuss is Fulton J. Sheen, who was the first Catholic televangelist. Sheen was the Emmy Award winning star of a television program that received high ratings and was watched by up to 30,000,000 Americans of all faiths in the 1950s. He was a Thomist scholar who believed that "faith depends on reason." In his 66 books, his 22 years of radio presentations on The Catholic Hour, and in his 127 television programs in his series, "Life Is Worth Living," Sheen used everyday examples, combined with history, logic and Catholic doctrine, to explore the myriad of problems of modern life in America in the 1950s. His mass audience appeal through the media, books, and other publications was augmented by his relentless, one-on-one, conversion outreach efforts, which led to the return, or conversion, to the Catholic faith of thousands of individuals, ranging from prominent public figures and American Communists to unknown people with whom Sheen would spend hours, days, and in some cases even weeks, educating them on the Catholic faith.

Fourth, we examine the influences of Catholicism on the work of singer and songwriter Bruce Springsteen. Springsteen's lyrics reflect his view that Catholic teachings reveal "a powerful world of potent imagery that became alive and vital and vibrant," and create an "incredible internal landscape." Springsteen sees his songs as confronting their characters with moral issues, and he seeks to provide them a map to address such issues. He therefore populates his songs with concrete characters facing the challenges of today's world, and often employs Catholic symbols and concepts in his lyrics. He acknowledges his debt to Flannery O'Connor, especially in the songs on his album "Nebraska," seeing her stories as exposing "some dark thing – a component of spirituality." Springsteen credits O'Connor with motivating him to "explor[e] characters of my own" because "She knew original sin — knew how to give it the flesh of a story." He sees his songs, at their core, as reflecting his own lifelong "search for faith and meaning," and concludes that "once you're a Catholic, there's no getting out."

Finally, we look at the religious poetry of two prominent twentieth century poets. Denise Levertov was born in England to a Jewish father who converted to Christianity and became an Anglican priest and an English Protestant mother who was descended from a famous Welsh mystic. Levertov moved to the United States after her marriage, becoming an American citizen in 1955. She wrote some twenty books of poems, and taught at several distinguished universities, including a tenured professorship at Stanford. Levertov was an agnostic for much of her life, and became a Catholic less than a decade before her death. Seeing poetry as a vocation and poems as "a form of prayer," she was influenced by Ignatius Loyola's *Spiritual Exercises* to write poems which focussed on gospel stories and Christ's Resurrection and Ascension, among other religious themes.

John Berryman was a better-known poet than Levertov, and won the Pulitzer Prize for Poetry in 1964. Like Leverov, he taught at the university level, mainly in his native state of Minnesota. Scarred by the suicide death of his father when Berryman was only twelve, he became an alcoholic, and married three times. After a prolonged stay at an alcohol rehabilitation institution, Berryman returned briefly to the Catholic faith of his youth and wrote "Eleven Addresses to the Lord" in his 1970 book of poems, *Love and Fame*. These "addresses" recognize the influence of God in his life, express thanks and doubts, and ask for continuing assistance, with a concluding hope for redemption, with Berryman praying that "I may be ready with my witness" through what may be "awarded" him, including "Cancer, senility, mania." Berryman relapsed within months, and committed suicide in 1972, jumping to his death from a Minneapolis bridge.

CHAPTER ONE

THE GRACE-FILLED WORLD OF FLANNERY O'CONNOR

> "Making grace believable to the contemporary reader is the almost insurmountable problem of the novelist who writes from the standpoint of Christian orthodoxy."
>
> Flannery O'Connor

Flannery O'Connor (1925-1964) was the preeminent American Catholic writer of the twentieth century. She burst upon the literary scene with her brilliant first novel, *Wise Blood*, in 1952 but was dead from lupus twelve years later. Her literary merit was recognized in many prizes, and she was honored in 1988 with a volume of her novels, short stories, letters and occasional prose published as part of the prestigious Library of America. When asked to compare her to other writers, Thomas Merton observed that "when I read Flannery I don't think of Hemingway, or Katherine Anne Porter, or Sartre, but rather of someone like Sophocles...for all the truth and all the craft with which she shows man's fall and his dishonor."

Catholicism pervades O'Connor's entire body of work. O'Connor described her Catholic beliefs in a 1962 letter to Alfred Corn, a young poet. She wrote that "I am a Catholic... [and] I believe what the Church teaches – that God has given us reason to use and that it can lead us toward a knowledge of him, through analogy; that he has revealed himself in history and continues to do so through the Church, and that he is present (not just symbolically) in the Eucharist on our altars. To believe all this I don't take any leap into the absurd. I find it reasonable to believe, even though these beliefs are beyond reason."

The Catholic concept of God's grace is an important element in O'Connor's work. She explained that all of her stories "are about the action of grace on a character who is not willing to support it," and, in her view, those stories are "guides… which affect our image and our judgment of ourselves. Abstractions, formulas, laws will not do here. We have to have stories….It takes a story of mythic dimensions; one which belongs to everybody; one in which everybody is able to recognize the hand of God and imagine its descent upon himself."

In this Chapter, we will look at three themes which repeat in O'Connor's work. These are (1) her empathy for the sick and disabled; (2) her scorn for those who looked at their religion as "the poor man's insurance system"; and (3) her use of sudden bursts of insight or illumination known as "epiphanies."

THE SICK AND DISABLED: "TEMPLES OF THE HOLY GHOST"

Born in Savannah, Georgia in 1925, Mary Flannery O'Connor spent most of her life, and went to college, in Milledgeville, Georgia. After receiving her undergraduate degree from the Georgia State College for Women, O'Connor enrolled in the Graduate Writing Program at the University of Iowa, receiving a Master of Fine Arts degree. She then went on to New York where she took up residence at the famous Yaddo artist colony in Saratoga Springs to pursue her writing, and then moved in with the Fitzgerald family in Ridgefield, Connecticut.

In her mid twenties, O'Connor was diagnosed with lupus, the degenerative disease which had killed her father at the age of 45. She returned to her family's farm in Milledgeville, with her health worsening, and walking only with crutches and pain. She was able to write only two to three hours a day, but bore her pain with acceptance. As she put it, "Sickness before death is a very appropriate thing and I think those who don't have it miss one of God's mercies." She characterized sickness as "a place, more instructive than a long trip to Europe, and it's always a place where there's no company, where nobody can follow."

O'Connor's stories often portray the sick, disabled, and marginalized as the exemplars who are saved, while the rich and powerful are doomed by their smugness unless they experience a redemptive epiphany. This canonization of the marginalized is well displayed in one of her early stories, "A Temple of the Holy Ghost" (1954), which illuminates the mystery of "the hand of God" working in a young girl's life through an unusual messenger.

The focus of the story is an unnamed twelve year old girl who is bright and religiously aware, but also "a born liar and slothful and she sassed her mother and was deliberately ugly to almost everybody. She was eaten up also with the sin of Pride, the worst one." Her mother and she are visited by two vapid cousins who call themselves "Temple One" and "Temple Two," mocking the nun at their convent school who told them to ward off boys' advances by proclaiming "Stop sir! I am a Temple of the Holy Ghost!" Rather than joining in the cousins' derisive giggles, the girl is pleased to think that she could be such a temple. "It made her feel as if somebody had given her a present."

The story ultimately proceeds to a country fair attended by the cousins, who return to tell the girl about a certain "freak" – a hermaphrodite – a circus attraction who exposes his/her dual nature separately to the men and women who pay to see the show. With dignity, the hermaphrodite cautions the fairgoers "God made me thisaway and if you laugh He may strike you the same way. This is the way He wanted me to be and I ain't disputing His way. I'm showing you because I got to make the best of it. I expect you to act like ladies and gentlemen. I never done it to myself nor had a thing to do with it but I'm making the best of it. I don't dispute hit."

Going to bed, the girl imagines the "freak" preaching sermon-like to the fairgoers that they and he/she are all Temples of the Holy Ghost. He tells them that "You! You are God's temple, don't you know? Don't you know? God's Spirit has a dwelling in you, don't you know? …. A temple of God is a holy thing. Amen. Amen. I am a temple of the Holy Ghost"

The next afternoon, the girl and her mother accompany the cousins back on their return to convent school. They go to the school's chapel where the girl kneels, realizing that she is in the presence of God. She begins to pray that she not be so mean or sass her mother, or talk like she does. As the priest lifts the consecrated host, her thoughts go back to the "freak" at the fair, who is saying "I don't dispute hit. This is the way He wanted me to be." When returning home, they find that the fair has been shut down because of complaints from the local preachers.

In a letter to a woman who questioned the meaning of the story, Flannery O'Connor wrote that there actually was a show at a local fair featuring a hermaphrodite, which she learned from her dairyman's daughter, and that the story was substantially the same as what O'Connor had been told by the daughter. The "point" of the story, she explained, "is of course in the resignation to suffering, which is one of the fruits of the Holy Ghost."

"A Temple of the Holy Ghost" teaches that every person has dignity and value in God's eyes. The girl's religious nature grasps this great truth about the "freak," a point the preachers cannot see. As a lonely and spiritual child, she realizes that the hermaphrodite has accepted the mystery of his/her suffering, thus giving the girl an ultimately redemptive and Christ-like example of acceptance.

CHRISTIAN ATHEISTS: THE GRANDMOTHER AND THE MISFIT

A self-described "hillbilly Thomist," O'Connor peopled her stories with strange figures from her native Protestant South who often terrorized "respectable" Protestant women who knew that God had chosen them to be saved among His elect. O'Connor explained that she needed such outsized figures because modern people are resistant to grace, and, as such, "for "the hard of hearing you shout, and for the almost-blind you draw large and startling figures."

Perhaps the strangest figure in O'Connor's stories is "The Misfit," who appears in her early and most famous short story, "A Good Man Is Hard to Find" (1953). This chilling story, which is often assigned reading for baffled private high school students, focuses on a self-centered, unnamed "Grandmother," who is on a car trip from Atlanta to Florida with her son and daughter in law, and their three children – a boy, a girl, and a baby. The grandmother resists the trip, using as one excuse the news reports of an escaped killer known as "The Misfit," who is reportedly also "headed toward Florida." The grandmother ultimately convinces her son to go off the main road in search of an old plantation she remembered visiting as a "young lady." Here they meet up with The Misfit and his two companions, and all, including the baby, are murdered.

The heart of the story is the interaction between the grandmother and The Misfit. She keeps repeating that she knows he is "a good man" who "wouldn't shoot a lady," and urges him to pray because "If you would pray…Jesus would help you." The Misfit recounts the sad tale of his life but rejects Jesus. As he sees it, if Jesus raised the dead, then the only choice is to "throw away everything and follow Him." But if He did not raise the dead, then the alternative is to "enjoy the few minutes you got left the best way you can – by killing somebody or burning down his house or doing some other meanness to him. No pleasure but meanness."

As The Misfit finishes, near tears, with his voice sounding "about to crack," "the grandmother's head cleared for an instant," and she reaches out to The Misfit, touching him on the shoulder while murmuring "Why you're one of my babies. You're one of my own children." The Misfit recoils from her touch and shoots her three times, observing to his companions that "She would have been a good woman...if it had been somebody there to shoot her every minute of her life."

The grandmother is the type of shallow believer that O'Connor found "repulsive" because people like her "really don't have faith but a kind of false certainty. They operate by the slide rule and the Church for them is not the body of Christ but the poor man's insurance system. It's never hard for them to believe because actually they never think about it." In short, "They think faith is a big electric blanket, when of course it is the cross." The grandmother is such a person; like the Pharisee in Luke's Gospel, she is the type of person that would thank God that she is not like the rest of humanity. She sees herself as "a lady," and overdresses for the car trip because "In case of an accident, anyone seeing her dead on the highway would know at once that she was a lady." Until her final moments, when her "head cleared for an instant," she is shallow and complacent, with only "superficial beliefs."

In his perceptive analysis of "A Good Man Is Hard to Find," Richard Giannone portrays the grandmother as a victim of her own self-will. Indeed, it was her mistaken belief about the location of the plantation, and her insistence that the family interrupt their trip to Florida to visit it, that led to the deaths of her entire family. Only her ultimate submission to The Misfit's will, and her display of compassion toward him, redeems her. In Giannone's words, "for the grandmother, life and death become meaningful when she answers the call for compassion that draws her closer to all that she has wished for in life." Once again, her reversal echoes the parable of the Pharisee and the tax collector, since, by humbling herself, she is exalted. At the end of the story, she lies dead, but her face is "smiling up at the cloudless sky."

Edward F. Mannino

Epiphanies: Ruby Turpin's "Revelation"

O'Connor's stories usually involve a protagonist who lives a shallow life, and is suddenly confronted, in a moment of grace, with a shocking and revelatory insight into that shallowness. These revelatory moments are known as "epiphanies," from the Greek word for "manifestation." Such a moment touches the grandmother in "A Good Man Is Hard to Find," when her head "cleared for an instant" and she reaches out and touches The Misfit, recognizing him as one of her children. O'Connor explained that "Her head clears for an instant and she realizes, even in her limited way, that she is responsible for the man before her and joined to him by ties of kinship which have their roots deep in the mystery she has been merely prattling about so far. And at this point, she does the right thing, she makes the right gesture...." Moreover, O'Connor continued, this epiphany for the grandmother will also become one for The Misfit because "the old lady's gesture, like the mustard-seed, will grow to be a great crow-filled tree in the Misfit's heart, and will be enough of a pain to him there to turn him into the prophet he was meant to become."

In "Revelation" (1963), one of her last short stories, O'Connor portrays another such shocking insight. This one changes the comfortable life of Ruby Turpin, one of the self-selected elect, "a respectable, hard-working, church-going woman." "Mrs. Turpin," as she is called throughout the story, has taken her husband Claud to a doctor's waiting room, where most of the story unfolds. Claud has been kicked in the leg by a cow on their farm, which was populated not only by cows, but also by eight hogs living in a "pig parlor." Mrs. Turpin surveys the waiting room, instantly classifying each of the waiting patients and their family members accompanying them into their proper group. As she saw it, there were ranks assigned to all people. At the bottom were the "colored people" and the "white trash," with the "home-owners" like she and Claud sitting above them. Highest on the "heap" were "people with a lot of money and much bigger houses and much more land." Mrs. Turpin gave thanks to Jesus for her own ranking, pleased that He had not "made her a n***er or white trash or ugly" like the college girl sitting with her mother in the waiting room, glaring at Ruby. As the story progresses,

Mrs. Turpin engages the other waiting patients in small talk which makes her social views obvious to all.

Suddenly, the small talk between the mother of the college girl and Mrs. Turpin, joined by Claud, turns to criticism of the girl, who continues to glare in silence at Ruby who prattles on and on about how lucky she is, telling the girl how it never hurts to smile. In a scene which calls to mind Saul of Tarsus being struck from his horse by God, Mrs. Turpin is struck in the head over her left eye by a book the college girl — whose name is Mary _Grace_ — has hurled at her. The girl jumps on her, sinking her fingers "into the soft flesh" of Ruby's neck. After peace is restored, Mrs. Turpin asks the girl "What you got to say to me?", "waiting, as for a _revelation_." The girl, Mary Grace, replies "Go back to hell where you came from, you old wart hog."

After returning to her farm, Ruby lies down, denying to herself that she is a wart hog from hell, but she cries, realizing that she – "a respectable, hard-working, church-going woman" – had been "singled out" for what was surely a "message." Going down to the pig parlor, Mrs. Turpin calls out to God, crying "What do you send me a message like that for? .... How am I a hog and me both? How am I saved and from hell too?" Continuing her fury at God, she finally yells "Go on...call me a hog! Call me a hog again. From hell. Call me a wart hog from hell. Put that bottom rail on top. There'll still be a top and a bottom."

The story ends with Mrs. Turpin's Pauline vision of "a vast horde of souls...rumbling toward heaven." But this horde marches in a different order than that into which she had classified the world. She sees "whole companies of white-trash, clean for the first time in their lives, and bands of black n***ers in white robes, and battalions of freaks and lunatics shouting and clapping and leaping like frogs. And bringing up the end of the procession was a tribe of people whom she recognized at once as those who, like herself and Claud, had always had a little of everything and the God-given wit to use it right...They were marching behind the others with great dignity, accountable as they had always been for good order and common sense and respectable behavior. They alone were on key. Yet she could see by their shocked and altered faces that even their virtues were being burned away." The story concludes with Ruby realizing that "what she had heard were the voices of the souls climbing upward into the starry field and shouting hallelujah."

In a letter explaining "Revelation" to Maryat Lee, a New York playwright/intellectual and frequent correspondent, Flannery O'Connor called Ruby's vision "purgatorial," and explained that Ruby "gets the vision." She is called to repent and to be purged of her prideful divisions of people into lower and upper classes. She had previously led an outwardly good life, but not one humble enough. Her "Revelation" is an epiphany which may ultimately lead to her salvation.

Flannery O'Connor's stories illustrate the manner in which God's grace transforms those who make the choice to accept it. As the Council of Trent taught, the gift of grace "sanctifi[es] and renovat[es] the inner person," who "ceases to be a sinner and 'becomes just'." So it was for the hermaphrodite and the schoolgirl, for the grandmother, and even for Mrs. Turpin.

CHAPTER TWO

THOMAS MERTON: AMERICA'S SPIRITUAL DIRECTOR

When Thomas Merton died prematurely at the age of 53, his obituary appeared on the front page of the *New York Times*. In an article written by Israel Shenker, the *Times* observed that Merton "was a writer of singular grace about the City of God and an essayist of penetrating originality on the City of Man." Merton was a polymath who authored more than 100 books and booklets, along with hundreds of poems and essays. In addition, he was an inveterate letter writer, who corresponded with famous novelists, poets, spiritual leaders, and ordinary people, including children. His essential gift to the American people, however, was his body of work on contemplation. His books and essays were meant to bring the practice of contemplation out of the monastery and into the lives of individual people living in the outside world of work, family and the noise and distractions of American life in the mid-20th century. Along with Bishop Fulton J. Sheen, whom we will discuss in the next chapter, Merton also brought Catholicism into the mainstream of American life in the era following World War II, helping to break down the historic Protestant distrust of all things Catholic.

Merton did all this while living the life of a contemplative monk at the Trappist Abbey of Gethsemani in Kentucky, which he entered on December 10, 1941, when he was 27. He died exactly 27 years later, on December 10, 1968, in a freak accident on his Asian journey, when he was electrocuted by a fan he touched when exiting the shower.

MERTON'S LIFE AND WORK

Thomas Merton was born in Prades, France on January 31, 1915, the oldest son of Owen and Ruth Merton. Owen was an artist who moved Thomas and his brother John Paul from country to country, after Ruth died of cancer when Thomas was only six years old. They lived off and on in France, Bermuda, England, and the United States, until Owen died when Thomas was 16. After Owen's death, Merton enrolled at Cambridge University in England in 1933. He left Cambridge abruptly, apparently as a result of fathering a child out of wedlock. In 1935, Merton enrolled at Columbia University in New York, from which he graduated in 1938. He edited the literary magazine at Columbia, and made several influential friends who remained so throughout his entire life. These included the editor and later publisher, Robert Giroux; the poet and mystic, Robert Lax; and the abstract painter, Ad Reinhardt. At Columbia, Merton was mentored by Mark Van Doren, who was responsible for getting Merton's first work, a book of poems, published. Van Doren remained close to Merton through correspondence for the rest of Merton's life.

Influenced by the poetry of William Blake and Gerard Manley Hopkins, as well as by Etienne Gilson's *Spirit of Medieval Philosophy*, Merton became a Catholic in 1938, when he was 23 years old. Worn out by the misery his prior dissolute life had caused him, and seeking both meaning and mortification, he soon began to consider the monastic life. Turned down by the Franciscans when he revealed his sins of the past, he found the Trappists after attending a retreat at Gethsemani.

Encouraged by his abbot, Merton worked on an autobiography which was published in 1948 as *The Seven Storey Mountain: An Autobiography of Faith*, a title taken from Dante's *Purgatorio*. Focusing on his conversion, his book became a major bestseller in 1949, curiously the same year in which Paul Blanshard's anti-Catholic polemic *American Freedom and Catholic Power* also appeared on the list of bestsellers. Merton's book sold 600,000 copies in hardcover and was the number three bestseller in 1949. Its popularity was explained partially by the war-weariness of the nation and Americans' need to find meaning after the depravities of World War II, including the Holocaust. Merton's autobiography reflected a fierce, militant, and insular Catholicism, which came to embarrass him in later years, when he became attracted to the insights of other religions, including both Zen Buddhism and Islam.

Merton was ordained as a priest in 1949, and became an American citizen in 1951. His interests broadened in the late 1950s and 1960s to include social issues. During this period, the contemplative monk became a social critic of war, nuclear weapons, and racism. As a contemplative, he gradually had become aware that he could serve the role of an active outsider who could objectively view modern society from a distance. In this way, he mirrored the experience of Dante, who had been exiled from his beloved city of Florence and who wrote *The Divine Comedy* while in exile.

Merton's social criticism was extensive. In the area of race relations, Merton supported Martin Luther King, and wrote four essays on race in 1963, published as "Letters to a White Liberal." He also became an antiwar spokesperson, and began writing for Dorothy Day's *The Catholic Worker*. He wrote powerful and original poems on Auschwitz ("Chants to be Used in Processions around a Site with Furnaces") and the atomic bomb dropped on Hiroshima ("Original Child Bomb"), as well as a series of "Cold War Letters," which were mimeographed and distributed by other peace activists, when Merton was forbidden to comment publicly on such issues. Merton opposed the burning of draft records by his friends, the Catholic priests and brothers, Daniel and Philip Berrigan, and ultimately resigned from the Catholic Peace Fellowship after a twenty-two-year-old Catholic Worker named Roger La Porte burned himself to death in an antiwar protest outside the headquarters of the United Nations in 1964. He observed that "This suicide business is surely demonic. God help us."

Merton was also both a traditional and experimental poet, and an astute literary critic. He wrote essays on a broad range of literary topics, including seven essays on the works of the brilliant agnostic Albert Camus, and essays on broad variety of other writers, including Flannery O'Connor, William Faulkner, James Joyce, Boris Pasternak, and a number of lesser-known Latin American poets.

In 1966, Merton became involved romantically with a student nurse in her twenties who had assisted Merton when he was hospitalized in Louisville, Kentucky. This affair lasted several months, but was broken off by Merton when he was forced by his abbot to choose between leaving or remaining at Gethsemani. During his remaining time at Gethsemani, he lived as a hermit on the monastery's property, a contemplative life which he had long sought.

Merton became increasingly interested in the insights of Eastern religions, especially Zen Buddhism. He wrote several works on the topic, and got permission to travel to Asia in 1968, to attend an interfaith world religions conference. He traveled to Asia in October of 1968, visiting India, Tibet, Ceylon, and Thailand. He met the Dalai Lama (who then was 33 years old), and visited a number of religious sites in India and Southeast Asia. His death by accidental electrocution occurred on December 10, 1968, which was 27 years to the day that he entered Gethsemani. Ironically, given his antiwar writings, his body was returned to the United States in a U.S. Army plane. His death by electrocution was also ironic, since his autobiography, *The Seven Storey Mountain*, ends with a meditation where God tells Merton that he will find the solitude he sought in order that "you may become the brother of God and learn to know the Christ of the burnt men."

MERTON'S WRITINGS ON CONTEMPLATION AND THE TRUE AND FALSE SELF

The Thomas Merton of *The Seven Storey Mountain* was a wounded individual fleeing from the snares of society to the safety of a monastic bubble. As he said later, "the conception of 'separation from the world' that we have in the monastery too easily presents itself as a complete illusion: the illusion that by making vows we become a different species of being, pseudoangels, 'spiritual men,' men of interior life, what have you." Merton escaped from this early insularity to fully embrace those in the outside world. His new view became crystallized by an experience in Louisville, Kentucky at the corner of Fourth and Walnut Streets in 1958. He wrote about this experience several times and, in his final meditation on it, commented that while walking in the center of Louisville's shopping district, he was overwhelmed by the sudden realization that he loved all the people surrounding him. He characterized the experience as "like waking from a dream of separateness, of spurious self-isolation in a special world, the world of renunciation and supposed holiness," a dream he had lived in for sixteen or seventeen years. Now he realized that there was no "separate holy existence," and that all people "belong to God."

Given this epiphany, Merton began years of writing on contemplation to assist those living outside the cloister in their daily lives. One of the principal concepts he advanced in his writings was that of the true and false self. He explained that "There is an irreducible opposition between the deep transcendent self that awakens only in contemplation, and the superficial, external self which we commonly identify with the first person singular." To find salvation, each individual must discover his or her true self. Finding our true self does not happen by emulating others. As Merton put it, "Many poets are not poets for the same reason that many religious men are not saints: they never succeeded in being themselves. They never get around to being the particular poet or the particular monk they are intended to be by God. They never become the man or the artist who is called for by all the circumstances of their individual lives. They waste their years in vain efforts to be some other poet, some other saint."

Each of us is different, for "No two created beings are exactly alike. And their individuality is no imperfection. On the contrary, the perfection of each created thing is not merely in its conformity to an abstract type but in its own individual identity with itself. This particular tree will give glory to God by spreading out its roots in the earth and raising its branches into the air and the light in a way that no other tree before or after it ever did or will do."

For Merton, the danger to those living in the everyday world came from the pressures to assume a collective identity, which forced them to wear what he referred to as "masks." Thus, we come to see ourselves as Americans or Germans, white or black, conservative or liberal, or as the embodiment of some general type. In Merton's view, this leads to alienation from our true self. He explained that "Alienation begins when culture divides me against myself, puts a mask on me, gives me a role I may or may not want to play. Alienation is complete when I become completely identified with my mask, totally satisfied with my role, and convince myself that any other identity or role is inconceivable. The man who sweats under his mask, whose role makes him itch with discomfort, who hates the division in himself, is already beginning to be free."

When we assume these other identities, and choose to wear the mask that accompanies them, we choose a false self, which Merton described as an "evanescent shadow" or a "smoke self." Contemplation helps us to realize this, assisting us to evade our selfish ego self, by shedding it like a snake sheds its skin. This shedding permits us to be reborn through contemplation, and awakened to the new life of the true self God wants us to become.

As Merton put it, "The only true joy on earth is to escape from the prison of our own false self, and enter by love into union with Life Who dwells and sings within the essence of every creature and in the core of our own souls."

Merton discussed these ideas in many books and booklets on contemplation. Most consider his finest work on contemplation to be *New Seeds of Contemplation*, which first appeared in 1962, as a complete rewriting of a 1949 book titled *Seeds of Contemplation*. In thirty-nine chapters, *New Seeds of Contemplation* treats a multitude of issues regarding contemplation. The separate chapters bear such titles as "What Is Contemplation?," "What Contemplation Is Not," "Everything That Is, Is Holy," "We Are One Man," "From Faith to Wisdom," "Integrity "," Faith," "Detachment," "Distractions," and "Sharing the Fruits of Contemplation."

MERTON'S INCARNATIONAL SPIRITUALITY

Merton also called on his readers to awaken to the beauty of the natural world and of the people in their lives. Like Flannery O'Connor, Merton's spirituality was incarnational, focusing upon the specifics of daily life, rather than upon abstract concepts. His writings, particularly in his journals and poems, document the splendors that are to be seen in our everyday surroundings, and teach his reader to awaken to this beauty as part of his or her spiritual development.

Merton had an experienced eye that captured the raw beauty of the natural world. He wrote that "The forms and individual characters of living and growing things, of inanimate beings, of animals and flowers and all nature, constitute their holiness in the sight of God.... The special clumsy beauty of this particular colt on this April day in this field under these clouds is a holiness consecrated to God by His own creative wisdom and it declares the glory of God. The pale flowers of the dogwood outside this window are saints. The little yellow flowers that nobody notices on the edge of the road are saints looking up into the face of God."

Merton was able to capture this beauty in uncommon places. In his poem, "The Trappist Abbey: Matins," for example, he writes of how he perceived the early morning abbey prayer experience at Gethsemani:

"When the full fields begin to smell of sunrise
And the valleys sing in their sleep,
The pilgrim moon pours over the solemn darkness
Her waterfalls of silence,
And then departs, up the long avenue of trees."

This unappreciated beauty is there to see not only in nature, but also in people. In his poem, "Elegy for a Trappist," for example, Merton captured the individual essence of an old monk who had spent his time, mostly unnoticed by his brother monks, tending the gardens at the abbey:

"Maybe the martyrology until today
Has found no fitting word to describe you
Confessor of exotic roses
Martyr of unbelievable gardens
Whom we will always remember
As a tender-hearted careworn
Generous unsteady cliff
Lurching in the cloister
Like a friendly freight train
To some uncertain station."

The poem continues by contrasting the quiet, gentle soul of this nearly invisible monk with the noise of modern life, from which he had hidden so well:

"In the dark before dawn
On the day of your burial
A big truck with lights
Moved like a battle cruiser
Toward the gate
Past your abandoned and silent garden
The brief glare
Lit up the grottos, pyramids and presences
One by one
Then the gate swung red
And clattered shut in the giant lights

43

And everything was gone
As if Leviathan
Hot on the scent of some other blood
Had passed you by
And never saw you hiding in the flowers."

In writings like these, Merton calls on his readers to awaken to such beauty in their daily lives. Like Gerard Manley Hopkins, whose poetry he admired, Merton saw the world as charged with the grandeur of God, and invited all to appreciate both the splendors of the natural world and the beauty of the individuals in each of our lives.

THOMAS MERTON, FIRE WATCHER

In his excellent survey of the mystical tradition in Catholicism and other religions, the Jesuit priest William Harmless titles his chapter on Merton "Mystic as Fire Watcher." The title is taken from Merton's famous meditation "The Fire Watch, July 4, 1952," in which Merton describes his duty as the night watchman who climbed a tower to watch for the fires that had long been a problem at Gethsemani. Harmless uses this meditation to encapsulate the role played by Merton in American life. As Harmless puts it, "The mystic, Merton implies, is to be a watchman, to alert us to the fires, to the dangers in our world, helping us see things we do not see because we are consumed by sleep." Moreover, "The mystic as fire watcher has another function: to help us recover our night vision, to see the beauty of our God-charged world."

Merton performed these functions well, writing against the evils of war and racism, documenting the raw materials of everyday beauty, and becoming a spiritual director for many Americans of differing faith traditions. He continues to fill this role today through his extensive writings, and also through the publications of the International Thomas Merton Society, and the booklets and retreats sponsored by the Merton Institute for Contemplative Living.

CHAPTER THREE

FULTON J. SHEEN: AMERICA'S CATHOLIC TELEVANGELIST

The Emmy Award for the Outstanding Television Personality of 1952 went to a Catholic priest. His television show was the most popular one in that year, beating out that of the comedian Milton Berle – "Mr. Television" himself. Remarkably, this award to a Catholic cleric came at a time when Paul Blanshard's anti-Catholic books were still best-sellers. By the time the show moved to the ABC network in 1955, it attracted some 30,000,000 viewers at the height of its popularity.

The Catholic priest was Bishop Fulton J. Sheen, and he reached more individuals with a message based on Thomistic Catholic thought than either Flannery O'Connor or Thomas Merton. Indeed, his activities through radio, television, books, and personal one-on-one efforts at saving souls were a major contributing factor in gaining acceptance for Catholics as true Americans in post World War II America.

SHEEN'S LIFE AND WORKS

Peter Sheen was born in Illinois in 1895. During grade school, for reasons still unknown, his name was changed from Peter to Fulton, his mother's maiden name. He was educated in Catholic grade and high schools, and then attended St. Viator College and Seminary in Illinois, graduating with both a Bachelor of Arts and a Master of Arts degree. His next educational stop was at St. Paul's Seminary, which was started by Archbishop John Ireland, the colleague of Cardinal Gibbons whom we met above, in the Prologue. Ordained a priest in 1919, Fulton Sheen then attended Catholic University in Washington, D.C., obtaining his S.T.L. and J.C.B. degrees from that institution in 1920.

45

Encouraged by his bishop, John Lancaster Spalding of Peoria, Illinois, who had attended the Catholic University of Louvain in Belgium, Sheen received his Ph.D. from that prestigious European university, which was one of the oldest in the world, in 1923. Always ambitious, Sheen realized that a European degree was a great asset for an American to have to assist in the hoped-for ascension up the various rungs of the Catholic Church hierarchy. Sheen performed to a high degree of excellence in his studies at Louvain, and became the first American to attain the prestigious *agrege* postdoctorate award, which made the recipient eligible to join the Louvain faculty. He toured throughout Europe during his studies, visiting many countries, including Italy, France and Greece. He next went on to England, teaching dogmatic theology for a brief period, and making more contacts, including the famous Catholic polemicist, G.K. Chesterton, who had his own weekly radio show. In time, one London newspaper would call Sheen "the American Chesterton."

Sheen's dissertation, with the imposing title, *God and Intelligence in Modern Philosophy,* was published in 1926 with an introduction from Chesterton. An intellectual tour-de-force, it won the Cardinal Mercier Prize for International Philosophy, an award which was given only once every ten years. He was the first American to be so honored.

Sheen's career thus started as a scholarly one. He was a Thomist, and was fond throughout his long life of remarking that "faith depends on reason." A voracious reader and acquirer of books on all subjects, Sheen taught at Catholic University in Washington, D.C. for 25 years, switching from the Theology to Philosophy Department due to personal disputes between him and other members of the Theology Department, some of whom questioned his scholarly credentials.

Sheen switched his focus early on from scholarly work to a more popular orientation to spiritual development for the Catholic in the pew, as well as fallen-away Catholics and non-Catholics as well. He wrote sixty six books, many of them hitting the same themes repetitively. Several became best sellers.

He became famous for his ability to convert people of all ages, classes, and faiths (or no faith at all), spending at times days and weeks working with people who struggled with atheism or other forms of unbelief. His more famous converts included Clare Boothe Luce, a former congresswoman and then wife of *Time* magazine publisher Henry Luce, auto magnate Henry Ford II, and several American communists. But his outreach also included hundreds of ordinary people, with whom he would spend whatever time was required to bring them back to God. Indeed, for the twenty five years he taught at Catholic University in Washington, D.C., he commuted each weekend to New York City to hold classes to instruct potential converts, with each class yielding 50 to 100 people who embraced the Catholic faith.

Sheen's many saintly features were marred by vanity and ambition. He lived quite well. Since he was not an order priest, he had not taken a vow of poverty and amassed a great fortune, which he gave away continuously in large and small amounts. But he drove Cadillacs, donated by an auto dealer, and lived in a luxurious mansion in Washington which was completed in 1941, and resold much later for over one million dollars. It had a recording studio, two studies, a very expensive air-conditioning system, and a private chapel. Sheen retained a cook, a gardener, and a driver/houseboy in residence.

His politics were generally conservative, characterized by the militant anti-Communism we discussed above in the Prologue. He was conversant with the details of communist theory, and regularly read all the communist publications, including *The Daily Worker*. His conservative friends included Al Smith, the first Catholic presidential candidate, who opposed the New Deal, and F.B.I. Director J. Edgar Hoover. Sheen saw the New Deal and Dorothy Day's Catholic Worker Movement as too utopian, and attacked the Supreme Court's school prayer and bible-reading decisions in testimony before the U.S. House of Representatives' Judiciary Committee in 1964. He also repeatedly denounced Freudian psychoanalysis for its denial of sin, and linked it with Marxism.

Sheen also had decidedly liberal views on some subjects. He preached regularly against racism and anti-Semitism, denounced the use of atomic weapons against Japan, and was the first notable Catholic cleric to call for immediate withdrawal of all U.S. troops from the Vietnam War.

While he supported the reforms of Vatican II and was a friend of Pope John XXIII, Sheen rejected much of the new bible scholarship, preferring to rely on a more literal reading of scripture, particularly in his books for the mass market.

SHEEN'S MEDIA CAREER

For over 25 years, Fulton Sheen was a popular speaker on radio and then television. His media career began in earnest as the featured speaker on The Catholic Hour radio program in 1930, which he continued to 1952, when he switched to television. The radio program reached four million listeners, many of whom were non-Catholic. Requests for transcripts of his talks sometimes numbered over 100,000, and Sheen received 3000 to 6000 letters per day.

Sheen is best remembered for his television program, "Life Is Worth Living," which ran from 1952 to 1957. He did 127 live programs, beginning on Tuesday, February 12, 1952, first on the old Dumont network, and then, starting in 1955, on ABC. The program moved to Thursday night at 8 p.m. when it switched networks. Life Is Worth Living reached 30,000,000 viewers at its peak in 1955, and Sheen received 15,000 to 25,000 letters each day during the series.

Sheen appeared in full ecclesiastical garb, including a flowing red cape, and a large red sash, with a prominent pectoral cross hanging from his neck. He gave unscripted talks, without notes or a teleprompter, and often wrote key phrases on a blackboard, which was erased during station breaks by his "angel." He prepared by developing detailed outlines, which he discarded before going on the air. In the first year, his competition came from television pioneer Milton Berle and a show starring Frank Sinatra, both of which lost the ratings battle to Sheen, who won the Emmy Award that year as the Outstanding Television Personality, and appeared on the cover of *Time* Magazine. When he accepted the Emmy Award, he thanked his writers – "Matthew, Mark, Luke, and John."

SHEEN'S SERVICE AND OFFICES IN THE CATHOLIC CHURCH

During his television series, Sheen also served as an auxiliary bishop in New York. He held that position from 1951 to 1966, and served simultaneously as national director of the Society for the Propagation of the Faith from 1950 to 1966. He donated his salary from Life Is Worth Living, which started at $26,000 per show, to the Society. Ultimately, Sheen gave approximately $10,000,000 to charity, with the funds coming from his royalties, fees, and many contributions which were given to him personally. His donations were made to many groups and individuals, ranging from the Society for the Propagation of the Faith, which received at least $1,000,000, to African-American missions and countless individuals in need.

Sheen reported to Francis Spellman, Cardinal of New York and the most powerful Catholic prelate in the United States. While never an admirer of Spellman, whom he considered to be an inferior intellect, Sheen got along well with Spellman until two incidents in the 1950s, which resulted in Life Is Worth Living being pulled from the air, when Spellman withdrew his approval for Sheen to continue the television program.

In the first incident, Spellman requested money from the Society for the Propagation of the Faith to distribute more free surplus food donated by the United States government for distribution to needy people in Europe. Sheen refused the request because of limited resources, and his refusal was supported by his Board. Spellman retaliated by appealing to Pope Pius XII to have Sheen removed as the Society's director, but the pope refused to do so.

The second incident also related to surplus food. Spellman requested the Society to reimburse him for the costs of that food, which in fact had been supplied free of charge by the government to be distributed to needy people in post war Europe. When Sheen again refused, Spellman again appealed to the pope, and both he and Sheen personally appeared before Pius to present their positions. Once again, the pope sided with Sheen, denying the request for "reimbursement" by Spellman.

As a result of these two incidents, Spellman began investigations into Sheen, which revealed no wrongdoing. Spellman then lobbied for Sheen's removal as auxiliary bishop, which ultimately was granted by Pope Paul VI, who appointed Sheen Archbishop of Rochester, New York, in 1956, when Sheen was 71 years old.

Sheen wanted to make Rochester a model Vatican II diocese, and made several attempts to do so with new appointments and programs. He made special efforts to fight a major problem of racial discrimination in the diocese, but his efforts were quite unpopular and his administrative skills meager. He resigned as archbishop in 1969, and returned to live in an apartment in New York City. For the remaining ten years of his life, he devoted his time to prayer, retreats, preaching, and writing. He died in his apartment chapel on December

9, 1979, at the age of 84. He had been working on his autobiography, which was published in 1980 as *Treasure in Clay*.

"LIFE IS WORTH LIVING": THOMISM FOR THE PEOPLE

The 127 episodes of Life Is Worth Living dealt with a multitude of topics covering virtually every area of modern life. Traditional religious topics, such as prayer, pain and suffering, conscience, character, and scripture were included, but so too were Communism, eastern religions, war, science, atomic weapons, work, love, sex, psychology and children. Here we discuss four of these programs as illustrations of Sheen's style and message.

1. "The Philosophy of Communism"

As we have noted both in the Prologue and in this Chapter, Fulton Sheen was an expert on Communism and attacked the underpinnings of its ideology using history, psychology, and logic. Several of his television programs were devoted to Communism and Russia, including the famous "Death of Stalin" presentation mentioned in the Prologue.

In "The Philosophy of Communism," Sheen characterized Communism as based upon two fallacies – economic determinism and a flawed "notion of man." Economic determinism was wrong as a principle since it confused the concepts of condition and cause. As Sheen explained, "the window is a *condition* of light, but the window is not the *cause* of light. We are willing to admit that economics, to some extent, does condition literature and art. But it certainly does not *cause* literature and art." He then went on to point out that different cultures and religions historically existed under the same economic methods of production, from the time of the Jews and Hindus and Chaldeans through Roman times, concluding that "Therefore, it is not economics that determines civilization. The way a violin is made does not determine the music that will be played on it." Here we have history, metaphor, and logic employed to teach through reason, as opposed to hyperbolic condemnation.

Turning to his second fallacy of Communism, Sheen noted that "The second basic principle of Communism is that man has value only inasmuch as he is a member of a class," and that it follows under that philosophy that "what happens to an individual person is of no concern." By contrast, the proper view is that every person has worth as a "creature of God." Sheen invoked the Declaration of Independence's recognition that "The Creator has endowed man with certain inalienable rights," and called on his viewers to recognize that the truth that each individual has intrinsic value is "the foundation stone of democracy." He concluded the program with the following peroration:

"Communists are right in saying this world needs a revolution, but not their cheap kind, which merely transfers booty and loot out of one man's pocket into another's. We need the kind of revolution that will purge out of a man's heart pride and covetousness and lust and anger....The Communist revolution has been a basic failure; it is not revolutionary enough; it leaves hate in the soul of man. We need not fear Communism as much as we need fear being Godless. If God is with us, then who can be against us?"

2. "Why Work is Boring"

In this presentation, Sheen dealt with the nature of work in an industrialized society, focusing upon the boredom which often accompanies repetitive work, such as that performed by workers in a factory making automobiles. In this type of work, the dignity of the worker is endangered. Sheen saw two ways — one economic, and the other spiritual — in which "the dignity of work may be restored."

Sheen's economic solution was one which drew on the teachings of the papal encyclicals dealing with social justice, starting with Leo XIII's *Rerum Novarum*, which we discussed in the Prologue. Sheen suggested that capital should give the laborer "some share in the profits or management or ownership of industry." He saw capital and labor not as foes, but as cooperating classes. He explained that "Capital and labor are classes, and no class is always right. We have suffered a great deal in the past from the evils of capital, and we could suffer a great deal from the evils of labor. Instead of being for either capital or labor, we should be for both. To ask, 'Which is more important?' is like asking which is more important to a man, his right leg or his left. Both! Capital and labor work together, producing for the common good; let both be responsible and both will have dignity, and the boredom will disappear."

Sheen went on to note that Christ himself both worked as a carpenter and "carpentered the universe itself." As such, Christ "is the only One in the world of Whom both capital and labor can say, 'He came from our ranks. He is one of our own.'"

Sheen then turned to the spiritual solution to workplace boredom. Invoking a common Catholic viewpoint that Thomas Merton would later echo in his writings, Sheen stated that "Mechanized work can be saved from drudgery by doing it with a Divine intention.... There is no work in the world that cannot be sanctified.... Whether we eat or drink or whatsoever we do, sanctification is possible when the task is offered in the name of God. We all have work to do that is unpleasant, but it becomes pleasant when we love someone. Work done for the love of God makes a man happier and gives him an inner peace the world cannot take away."

In this presentation on the very practical subject of work, we see Sheen incorporating the teachings of papal encyclicals on human dignity and social justice, as well as the writings over hundreds of years of Catholic contemplatives, but he does not present the ideas as Catholic beliefs. Instead, he explains them; he does not dogmatize.

3. "Reparation"

At the end of his presentation on "Reparation," Sheen called on President Eisenhower to "declare a National Day of Prayer and Penance," to "ask God for pardon and forgiveness" for America's sins. In the midst of the Cold War, Sheen explained that "World suffering and world crisis are... related to guilt, and guilt needs reparations, or the righting of wrong."

Using the image of the invisible "angel" that erased his blackboard, Sheen said that if he stole the angel's halo and then apologized for it, the angel would still require that Sheen give the halo back. Similarly, "A nation may do wrong; if so, it must make up for it by some kind of penance and atonement and reparation."

Invoking, as he often did, American history, Sheen turned to the experience of the Civil War and the leadership of Abraham Lincoln as president. Sheen explained that "National penance is a true American doctrine as well as a profound religious doctrine in the great Hebraic-Christian tradition. Lincoln expressed this better than any President our glorious country has ever had. Maybe he knew it because he was better schooled in sacrifice and suffering." Sheen went on to review many incidents from Lincoln's Civil War experience which left him exhausted and discouraged, concluding that "Out of this life of sorrow, misjudgment, trial, and war, a great character was made. His Calvaries enabled him to have an insight into the spiritual needs of a nation that is given to but a few."

The lessons from Lincoln's experience led him to call upon the American people, in his second inaugural address, to make reparations for their "national sins" in permitting the existence of slavery. In Sheen's view, similar reparations were called for in his time. "Would it not be well to let ring through America today a voice like Lincoln's, summoning us to fall prostrate before God and ask God for pardon and forgiveness." He ended with a quote from Lincoln: "It behooves us then, to humble ourselves before the Offended Power, to confess our national sins, and to pray for clemency and forgiveness."

In explaining the need for national repentance and reparation, Sheen thus utilized the American historical experience of one of our greatest presidents, rather than Catholic teaching, to support his call for prayer and penance. His approach was non-denominational, and welcoming to all.

Sheen's call for a National Day of Prayer and Penance was heard by President Eisenhower, who issued a Proclamation in June of 1953 for a "National Day of Penance and Prayer" to be held on the Fourth of July that year.

4. "Pain and Suffering"

When Sheen turned to the issue of pain and suffering, he separated his presentation into three parts, discussing what pain and suffering does to us; how to meet it; and why there is suffering. First, pain and suffering turn our focus inward, and can result either in selfishness leading to bitterness, or in self-examination, which can result in liberating individuals from that selfishness. Second, Sheen reviewed how various religious traditions answer the question of how to deal with pain and suffering. Stoics attempt to bear it, while Buddhists teach that pain and suffering are the result of desire, and therefore counsel individuals to work to extinguish all desires in their lives. Under the "Hebraic-Christian philosophy," by contrast, pain is seen as something to be transcended. How? Sheen explained that "Suffering is transcended through love." Although love cannot extinguish pain, it can diminish it. Using an example from the life of his viewers, he pointed to a mother who "sits up all night with a fever-stricken child." She does not see the experience as one of suffering, but rather one of "love and sacrifice."

Finally, Sheen turned to the thorny question of why there is suffering. After an exegesis of the Book of Job, he invoked the sacrifice of Christ on the cross to explain the meaning of suffering. By his suffering, Christ "walked through the forest first and showed us that without Good Friday there would be no Easter Sunday." In other words, suffering changes us and readies us for a new life, freed from the selfishness that existed in our former way of life.

Again, this is all traditional Catholic teaching, but presented in a non-denominational, "Hebraic- Christian" fashion.

GOD'S HOUND: BRINGING FAITH THROUGH REASON

Fulton Sheen often quoted Francis Thompson's poem, "The Hound of Heaven." In that poem, the narrator recounts how he fled from God "down the labyrinthine ways/Of my own mind; and in the mist of tears/I hid from him." At the end of the poem, however, God reaches out his hand and says, "Ah, fondest, blindest, weakest,/I am He Whom thou seekest!" Thompson's life story puts his poem in context. He was a medical student who became a heroin addict. He was saved by the intervention of the editor of an English periodical who took him to the Norbertine Abbey in Storrington, England, where he regained his health, conquering his addiction. In short, God had not given up on him.

In the terms of Thompson's poem, Sheen can be seen as God's own hound, seeking to reach and reclaim souls who had lost their faith or never had it to begin with. Sheen pursued such souls relentlessly, both on an individual basis as we saw above, and also on a mass basis through his addresses on radio, his television programs, and his sixty six books.

As befit a Thomist philosopher, Sheen sought to persuade his potential converts through reason, rather than through fear. In opposing the false god of Communism, for example, Sheen attempted to point out how its foundational principles were contradicted by history and logic. Similarly, he invoked the experience of the American Civil War and the sufferings of Abraham Lincoln to illustrate the need for Sheen's America to make reparations for its national sins, as America had been called to do by Lincoln for the national sin of permitting slavery to exist. In discussing the problems of boredom at work, he advocated an economic solution based on papal encyclicals which encouraged partnership between capital and labor, and he explained the basic concept in simple terms, using a metaphor comparing capital and labor to the two legs of a single human body. He also invoked everyday experiences in his presentations, as in explaining suffering and sacrifice. There he used the example of a mother staying up all night with a sick child. That was not seen as suffering by the mother, but rather as an expression of love and sacrifice.

In his television shows, as well as on the radio and in his writings, Fulton Sheen presented a logical and historically-based religion that was non-denominational on the surface but supported in its foundations by traditional Catholic teachings. By this approach and his very visible Catholic priestly mode of dress, Sheen helped make Catholics part of the American mainstream.

CHAPTER FOUR

BRUCE SPRINGSTEEN: THE SEARCH FOR FAITH AND MEANING IN A TROUBLED WORLD

"In the context of religion...as an exercise of the metaphor-making dynamisms, Bruce Springsteen's album "Tunnel of Love" may be a more important Catholic event in this country than the visit of Pope John Paul II."

Father Andrew Greeley, 1988

Bruce Springsteen is one of the world's leading entertainers and most prominent songwriters. He has sold over 120 million albums worldwide, and has won innumerable awards. Those awards include twenty Grammys, two Golden Globes, two Emmys, and one Academy Award for best song. He was named one of *Time Magazine's Most Influential People* in 2008, and is a member of The Rock and Roll Hall of Fame and the New Jersey Hall of Fame. In 2009, he was honored by the Kennedy Center for exemplary lifetime achievement in the performing arts.

SPRINGSTEEN'S LIFE AND CAREER

Bruce Springsteen was born on September 23, 1949, in Long Branch, New Jersey. While his last name is Dutch, his ancestry was a mixture of Italian, Irish, and Dutch. He had a strained relationship with his father, and an unhappy experience in his early schooling at St. Rose of Lima Catholic grade school in Freehold Borough, New Jersey. He recalls that "in the third grade a nun stuffed me in a garbage can under her desk because she said that's where I belonged." He also recalls being knocked down by a priest for a mistake he made while serving

Mass. Springsteen was rebellious as a teenager and did not fit in, particularly in school. He dropped out of a local college after a year.

Springsteen has experienced many ups and downs in his personal and professional life. While he began playing the guitar at the age of thirteen, he played with several groups in his early career in New Jersey, but did not achieve any meaningful success until his 1975 album, "Born to Run." That album led to widespread recognition, including Springsteen's appearance on the covers of both *Time* and *Newsweek* in October of 1975.

His personal life has also been filled with challenges. He married actress and model Julianne Phillips in 1985, but she filed for divorce in 1988, after Springsteen began an affair with Patti Scialfa, a singer with his famous E Street Band. Springsteen and Scialfa married in 1991, after the birth of their first son, and during her pregnancy with their only daughter. Springsteen's three children by his second marriage are now young adults, with two presently attending college.

SPRINGSTEEN'S SPIRITUALITY

It has long been recognized that Springsteen's songwriting is significantly affected by his Catholic upbringing. In the early part of his career, however, he publicly rejected religion. He said during his early career that he "quit the stuff when I was in eighth grade," and called religion "too ludicrous to go along with" after you are "older than thirteen." Gradually, Springsteen came to change his mind, seeing his Catholic education as unveiling "a powerful world of potent imagery that became alive and vital and vibrant, and was both very threatening and held out the promise of ecstasies and paradise. There was this incredible internal landscape that they created for you."

Springsteen's songwriting is often colored by Catholic symbols and a Catholic worldview. His songs often invoke specifically Catholic practices. In "I'll Work for Your Love," for example, he mentions the stations of the cross and the rosary, along with more general Christian symbols, including the cross and Jesus' crown of thorns. Commenting on his song, "Mary's Place," Springsteen noted that "I'm sure it's the Catholic coming out in me." Springsteen summed up his Catholic worldview in a recording session with VH1 in 2005, when he said "once you're a Catholic, there's no getting out."

Many of Springsteen's songs focus upon workers in their daily lives. He sings of a blue-collar worker's hopes and dreams, search for happiness and multiple disappointments. This is the same particularized, incarnational focus that we saw in the works of Flannery O'Connor and Thomas Merton. Springsteen says that in his songs, "The characters are confronting the questions that everyone is trying to sort out for themselves, their moral issues, the way those issues rear their heads in the outside world." In his view, his songs provide what he refers to as a "map" for himself and for his audience to address those issues. Springsteen sees himself as a writer, and considers writers to be "the canary [in the coal mine] for the larger society."

Springsteen wants his songs to present ideas and to ask "fundamental moral questions." He wants to "move those questions from the aesthetic into the practical, into some sort of action in the community or action in the way you treat your wife, or your kid, or speak to the guy who works with you." Given this view of his songwriting, it is not surprising that Springsteen has become politically active, having campaigned most recently on behalf of Barack Obama's successful presidential bid in 2008.

Springsteen acknowledges that he has been deeply influenced in his songwriting by Flannery O'Connor. In an interview with novelist Walker Percy's son, Will, in 1997, Springsteen said that "The really important reading that I did began in my late twenties, with authors like Flannery O'Connor. There was something in those stories of hers that I felt captured a certain part of the American character that I was interested in writing about. They were a big, big revelation.... There was some dark thing — a component of spirituality — that I sensed in her stories, and that set me off exploring characters of my own. She knew original sin — knew how to give it the flesh of a story."

Walker Percy had written Springsteen what he referred to as "a fan letter - of sorts" in 1989, which Springsteen did not reply to at the time. Percy noted that he had read an article in which Springsteen was identified as a Catholic and as an admirer of Flannery O'Connor. Percy told Springsteen in the letter that he was "interested in your spiritual journey," and wanted to know if there was "any other material about it."

Writing to Walker Percy's widow eight years later, Springsteen mentioned that Percy had written to him, and expressed his regrets for not having answered the correspondence. In his letter to Mrs. Percy, Springsteen explained his work in the following terms: "The loss and search for faith and meaning have been at the core of my own work for most of my adult life."

SPRINGSTEEN'S SONGS

The theme of loss, and of search, for both faith and meaning recurs throughout many of Springsteen's songs. His troubled relationship with his father surfaces in many of his songs, which also can be read more broadly in religious terms. In both "My Father's House" and "Wages of Sin," for example, Springsteen repeats the imagery of "trying to make it home through the forest before the darkness falls," "With the devil snappin' at my heels." When he finally arrives at his father's house, the door is closed and a woman he doesn't recognize tells him, "I'm sorry, son, but no one by that name lives here anymore."

"My Father's House" ends with the house standing "like a beacon calling me in the night" and "Shining 'cross this dark highway where our sins lie unatoned." And, in "Wages of Sin," he repeats this theme of an unsuccessful search for forgiveness, crying out that "I keep paying/Wages of sin for some wrong that I've done." These songs bring to mind both Thomas Wolfe's *You Can't Go Home Again*, and Don McLean's song, "American Pie," where "the three men I admire most, the Father, Son and Holy Ghost, took the last train to the coast, the day the music died."

This sense of failure and loss also appears in "Dead Man Walking," a Springsteen song about a condemned man awaiting execution. While that man was "born and christened" in "St. James Parish," he tells the nun who is helping him avoid execution that "Sister I won't ask for forgiveness/ My sins are all I have."

Springsteen's vision became even darker in his 1982 album, "Nebraska," where the title song is narrated by the serial killer Charles Starkweather on death row. Springsteen explained that he wrote the song because "Every one knows what it's like to be condemned." Starkweather, accompanied by his girlfriend, Caril Fugate, went on a murder rampage in the Midwest in the 1950s, killing eleven people.

Springsteen told Will Percy that he was "deep into O'Connor" at the time he wrote "Nebraska," and the final lines of the song echo those of The Misfit in O'Connor's story, "A Good Man Is Hard to Find." The Misfit recounts that there is "No pleasure but meanness," while Starkweather says ,"They wanted to know why I did what I did/ Well sir I guess there's just a meanness in this world."

Each of these songs explores man's fall and the loss of both faith and meaning. Their darkness begins to lift in songs such as "Reason to Believe." In that song, the theme of loss continues in verses which recite the tragedies of an abandoned spouse, a groom left at the altar, and the deaths of an elderly man and a dog. But hope emerges after each tragedy, since each story in the song ends with the refrain, "at the end of every hard earned day people find some reason to believe." Indeed, even "Dead Man Walking" ends on an up note, with the condemned man observing that "There's a new day comin'/And my dreams are full tonight."

Other Springsteen songs continue an uplifting and redemptive theme. As Andy Whitman has pointed out, "God shows up through the tangible means of redemptive human connections, through commitment and faithfulness, through the miracle of new life." Springsteen's songs examine individual lives and the challenges of troubled relationships, with hopes of ultimate redemption.

One good example of such a song is "Living Proof," which celebrates the redemptive force of the birth of a child. Springsteen sees his newborn son as "a little piece of the Lord's undying light," with a beauty "Like the missing words to some prayer that I could never make." The birth becomes redemptive to the father, who says that "Looking for a little bit of God's mercy/I found living proof."

Springsteen's vision of the promise of ultimate redemption culminates in the beauty of his song, "Jesus Was an Only Son." That song speaks both of the love of a mother for her child, and also of divine love for all mankind and the promise of redemption. In the song, Jesus, while dying on the cross, thinks of his life that could have been ("a loss that can never be replaced/A destination that can never be reached") but consoles his mother by kissing her hands and whispering, "Mother, still your tears,/For remember the soul of the universe/Willed a world and it appeared." In his VH1 Storytellers performance, Springsteen reinforces the theme of the song by observing that "Without compassion, we lose our only claim to divinity."

In the words of Ralph Woods, Bruce Springsteen is "Christ-haunted." His songs resonate with Catholic themes and symbols, documenting his upward journey searching for faith and meaning within the challenges and joys of daily life. As Father Andrew Greeley puts it, Springsteen is one of the "Catholic minstrels" who "revive and renew the fundamental religious metaphors." Many of his songs thus reach out and grab the deep longings of every person for wholeness, for meaning, and for redemption.

CHAPTER FIVE

DENISE LEVERTOV AND JOHN BERRYMAN: THE POET'S RELIGIOUS IMAGINATION

"When you're really caught up in writing a poem, it can be a form of prayer"

Denise Levertov

Denise Levertov and John Berryman were two prominent American poets of the twentieth century. Both received major poetry awards. Berryman won the Pulitzer Prize for Poetry and Levertov received the Robert Frost Medal for "distinguished lifetime service to American poetry." They each published multiple books of poems, and taught at prestigious universities. While their lives and literary styles differed widely, both wrote religious poems, Levertov throughout her life, and Berryman at the end of his. Levertov was an agnostic who turned to Christianity, and became a Catholic in her mid-sixties. Berryman was a cradle Catholic, who lost his religion early in life after his father's suicide when Berryman was only twelve years old. Berryman experienced a reconversion after a hospitalization for alcoholism, but relapsed again, committing suicide less than two years later. This chapter first reviews the life and careers of both poets, and then turns to their poems treating religious subjects.

DENISE LEVERTOV

Denise Levertov was born in London, England, in 1923. Her father Paul was a Russian Jew who converted to Christianity and became an Anglican priest. Her mother Beatrice was an English Protestant, and a descendant oof the well-known Welsh mystic, Angel Jones. Both parents were active in humanitarian efforts to assist Jewish and other refugees fleeing Hitler's Germany, and in efforts to promote human rights more generally. Levertov saw herself as socially isolated, with Jews seeing her as gentile, and gentiles seeing her as Jew. She was home-schooled and studied ballet, hoping in her younger years to become a ballerina. In World War II, Levertov served as a nurse and received a nursing degree.

Levertov began writing poems as a teenager, and sent some of her work to T.S. Eliot, who wrote back to encourage her to continue her efforts. Her first book of poems, *The Double Image*, was published in 1946, and followed the English neo-romantic style of that era. Her life and career changed dramatically when she married an American writer, Mitchell Goodman, and emigrated with him to the United States in 1948. She became an American citizen in 1955.

The author of some twenty books of poems, and three books of essays, Levertov taught at Brandeis, Tufts, and MIT on the East Coast, and at Stanford and the University of Washington on the West Coast. She moved to Seattle in 1989, and taught at both Stanford, where she was a full professor, and part-time at the University of Washington until she retired from Stanford in 1993.

True to her family heritage, Levertov was politically active, opposing the Vietnam War and demonstrating for nuclear disarmament, even serving short stints in jail for civil disobedience, mirroring similar experiences of another Catholic convert, Dorothy Day. She also served as Poetry Editor for the liberal magazine, *The Nation*.

Levertov saw poetry as a vocation. Susan Zeuenberger characterizes her view of the poet as "a priestly one," with the poet serving as "the mediator between ordinary people and the divine mysteries." Levertov's poetry is extremely incarnational, closely exploring the beauty of everyday experiences, from walking a dog to observing a flower, and examining the life of the spirit. She employs simple words and images, which are always concrete, and invites the reader to search their own experiences. Levertov is very approachable, a poet for all, not only for the cognoscenti. In a Memorial Resolution, her colleagues at Stanford praised her for "her extraordinary gifts of diction and rhythm and structure, and her idiosyncratic fusion of mystery and ordinariness." Joan Hallisey sees Levertov's poetry as combining a "strong blend of the mystical with a firm commitment to social issues."

Levertov's style was influenced by three major poets – Ranier Maria Rilke, William Carlos Williams, and Wallace Stevens. She recalled that Williams befriended her, and had a "very immediate and imitative" influence, opening up "a new way of handling language." She also saw Williams as having "a Franciscan sense of wonder." Stevens was seen by her to be a "very musical poet." She incorporated both the wonder and the music in her best poetry.

Levertov became a Catholic in 1989, less than a decade before her death in 1997, at the age of 74 from complications of lymphoma. She saw her religious poems as ones which "trace my own slow development from agnosticism to Christian faith, a movement incorporating much of doubt and questioning as well as of affirmation." Her Stanford colleagues observed that "the mystery of the Christian incarnation linked and grounded her sense of communal love and the continuous sacrament of experience." Levertov can be seen as linked to the seventeenth century Metaphysical Poets, and she wrote several poems in honor of one of them, the Anglican priest, George Herbert. In "The Thread," she reworks Herbert's famous poem, "The Pulley," with both poems visualizing God as tugging the poet to salvation.

In her final interview, Levertov explained that she began to write "explicitly Christian poems" because she thought that "interest in religion is a counterforce to the insane, rationalist optimism that surrounds the development of all this new technology…Our ethical development does not match our technological development." She also saw poetry as "a form of prayer," and "a religious experience."

THE STREAM & THE SAPPHIRE

Many of Levertov's religious poems are collected in *The Stream & the Sapphire: Selected Poems on Religious Themes* (1997). These poems embody Levertov's view that *The Spiritual Exercises* of Ignatius Loyola, the founder of the Jesuit Order, closely parallel how a poet or novelist imagines a particular scene. Her poems are a form of *lectio divina* ("divine reading"), taking the reader into the experience of some gospel reading, visualizing the Crucifixion, post-Resurrection appearances to the Apostles, the descent into hell, the Ascension, the Annunciation, the Incarnation, and even parables of Christ.

In "The Servant-Girl at Emmaus," Levertov takes us into the story related in Luke's Gospel (24:13-35) by reflecting on Diego Velazquez's painting "The Supper at Emmaus." Levertov invites her reader to witness the experience of "a young black servant intently listening" who sees the risen Christ dining with two of his disciples at Emmaus. They do not recognize Christ, but she does. She "listens" to their conversation and recognizes Christ as "the one who had looked at her...as no one had ever looked" at a prior time, during his public ministry. Only she "sees/the light around him/and is sure" He is the Christ. The poem recreates not just the scene, but the experience of the girl. The use of a young black female who is the first to recognize the risen Christ reflects both Levertov's feminism and her identification with ordinary people.

Levertov wrote several poems on the Crucifixion, including "On a Theme from Julian's Chapter XX," a reflection on Christ's suffering based upon the writings of the fourteenth and fifteenth century English mystic Julian of Norwich. Julian was a favorite subject for Levertov, and she was deeply influenced by her mystical insights. Levertov recreates the experience of the crucifixion with stark detail, picturing "Six hours outstretched in the sun, yes,/hot wood, the nails, blood trickling/into the eyes." Drawing on her experience as a nurse, Levertov continues the concrete imagery by comparing the sufferings of Christ on the cross to "a child/dazed in the hospital ward they reserved for the most abused." Christ is seen as the "King of Grief," opened "utterly to the pain of all minds, all bodies/...from the first beginning to the last day." In His suffering, Christ "took to Himself/ the sum total of anguish and drank/even the lees of that cup" and "sorrowed in kinship" with all humans, past, present, and future.

In "What the Figtree Said," Levertov recreates the parable of the withered figtree through the novel vantagepoint of the tree itself. Seeing itself as "helplessly barren," the figtree knows that "my day had come. I served/Christ the Poet,/who spoke in images." Its barrenness was "a metaphor for their failure to bring forth what is within them." The figtree's "absent fruit/stood for their barren hearts."

In one of her greatest religious poems, "Agnus Dei," Levertov calls on us to reflect on what it means to call Christ the "Lamb of God."

The lamb is depicted as a naïve and helpless creature, and hardly a divine being. It is a "leaper in air for delight of being, who finds in astonishment/four legs to land on." God is seen as "defenseless," with His "Omnipotence...tossed away." We are called to realize that it is we who "must protect this perversely weak animal" and "hold to our icy hearts a shivering God." By inviting us to imagine our relationship with God in a new way, seeing ourselves as helper to the Almighty, Levertov makes us feel the meaning of a metaphor we have heard forever, but saw only as signifying Christ as sacrifice.

JOHN BERRYMAN

John Berryman is about as far as humanly possible different from Denise Levertov, both in his poetry and his lifestyle. Born John Smith in Oklahoma in 1914, Berryman was the son of a banker father and a schoolteacher mother. His life was unalterably changed by the suicide of his father when Berryman was only twelve years old. In his poem, "Dream Song #145," Berryman narrates that his father shot himself "outdoors by my window."

When his mother remarried, Berryman was given his stepfather's surname. He attended Columbia College, where he overlapped for one year with Thomas Merton, and graduated in 1936. Berryman was an English major, studying under Mark Van Doren, who was also Merton's mentor. Berryman won both election to Phi Beta Kappa and a fellowship at Cambridge, which he attended for two years.

Berryman was a major figure among American "Confessional Poets," although he resisted such categorization. His life provides a prime example of Levertov's observation that "Back when Robert Lowell and Anne Sexton were the models for neophytes, you had to have spent some time in a mental hospital to qualify as a poet." Berryman was an alcoholic who fought depression after his father's suicide and attempted suicide himself when he was seventeen. He was hospitalized for alcoholism and related health problems in every year from 1959 to his death in 1972. Married three times, Berryman had a history of continuous infidelity. He committed suicide on January 7, 1972, by jumping from the Washington Avenue Bridge in Minneapolis.

Berryman won the Pulitzer Prize for Poetry in 1964 for his work

"77 Dream Songs," and was elected to the American Academy of Arts and Sciences in 1967. In 2004, the Library of America published an edition of his Selected Poems. He taught principally at the University of Minnesota, but also at Harvard, Brown, the University of California at Berkeley, and at the famous Iowa Writer's Workshop.

"Eleven Addresses to the Lord"

Berryman was baptized a Catholic, and served as an altar boy from the age of five, but relapsed from that faith after his father's suicide. In 1970, after one of his hospital stays for alcohol rehabilitation, he underwent a religious awakening, and proclaimed himself to be a Catholic again. During this time, he wrote a series of "Eleven Addresses to the Lord," his one attempt at religious verse. They appeared in his 1970 book of poems titled *Love & Fame*. His reconversion did not last, and he even denied that the "Eleven Addresses" were Christian poems. He committed suicide less than two years later.

In "Eleven Addresses to the Lord," Berryman recognizes that God has reached out to save him throughout his life. He sees God as "Master of beauty, craftsman of the snowflake/inimitable contriver" who has "come to my rescue again and again." He observes that "You have allowed my brilliant friends to destroy themselves/and I am still here, damaged but functioning."

Berryman announces that he is "Under new management, Your Majesty:/Thine. I have solo'd mine since childhood, since/my father's suicide when I was twelve/blew out my most bright candle faith, and look at me." What followed was not pretty – "Wives left me./Bankrupt I closed my doors. You pierced the roof/twice & again. Finally you opened my eyes." He asks in "A Prayer for the Self," "Who am I worthless that You spent such pains/and take may [sic] pains again?"

Berryman asks for continuing help. "Forsake me not when my wild hours come" and "When all hurt nerves whine shut away the whiskey."Despite his recognition that God has saved him, Berryman still expresses doubts. "If I say Thy name, art Thou there? It may be so."

Berryman expresses hopes for his final redemption, whatever may come in his future life. "May I stand until death forever at attention/

for any your least instruction or enlightenment/I even feel sure you will assist me again, Master of insight & beauty." He closes "Eleven Addresses to the Lord" with the following plea:

> "Make too me acceptable at the end of time
> In my degree, which then Thou wilt award.
> Cancer, senility, mania,
> I pray I may be ready with my witness."

CONCLUSION

Different as they were, both Denise Levertov and John Berryman display the influence of their Catholic faiths in the religious poetry they wrote. Berryman started his life as a Catholic and an altar boy, while Levertov followed a long road on her pilgrimage from agnosticism to Catholicism. Poems like those we have reviewed are, as Levertov observed, a form of prayer, and give an immediacy to the experience of faith, much like the epiphanies Flannery O'Connor wrote about. Whether we look at the poems recreating gospel stories in Levertov's work, or at the poems of Berryman, which encapsulate a *cri du' coeur*, they function like the Ignatian *Spiritual Exercises* to awaken the life of the spirit. They demonstrate the wisdom of Samuel Johnson's comment that a poem should not leave the reader as the poet found him or her.

PART III

CATHOLICS IN AMERICAN

PUBLIC LIFE

INTRODUCTION

In this part, we review the careers of three individuals from Catholic backgrounds who were active participants in the American political process in the twentieth century. Each of them drew on his Catholic education and training to inform his political views, and formulate his public policies. In their work, we see concern for the poor, for the immigrant, for minorities, for the human dignity of all, and for the common good. We also see a strong vision of federalism, emphasizing the need for local formulation of public policy, in conformity with the Catholic social justice teaching known as subsidiarity.

We start with Alfred E. Smith, the first Catholic candidate of a major political party for the American presidency. Smith was a four-term governor of New York, and was identified politically with urban America and its immigrant population. In New York politics, Smith was an advocate for increased legal protections for workers, including measures to insure industrial safety. He also sponsored legislation to increase funding for education and public health, as well as to provide more and better housing. Smith was an advocate for civil liberties for all, and fought against Progressive laws which would bar socialists from political office and "Americanize" immigrants. He incurred the wrath of the Ku Klux Klan for both his Catholicism and his opposition to Prohibition and restrictions on immigration. The vocal and virulent opposition of the Klan assured his loss to Herbert Hoover in the 1928 presidential campaign, in which Smith was the Democratic Party's first Catholic nominee.

We next turn to Michael Harrington, a fallen-away Catholic who became a major leader of the American Socialist movement. While Harrington lost his Catholic faith, he continued to credit it for his devotion to reforming society and protecting its most poor and vulnerable members. His brand of socialism encouraged active participation in the political process, and he worked within the Democratic Party to advance the candidacies of liberal politicians, including Robert and Ted Kennedy, Walter Mondale, and Jesse Jackson, who shared his views regarding assisting the poor, and providing employment for all. Harrington is best remembered for his 1962 book, *The Other America*, which documented the pervasive impact of poverty on some twenty-five percent of the American population, urban and rural, black, white, and Latino, young and old. His work sparked the War on Poverty, which was conceived by President John Kennedy and implemented by President Lyndon Johnson. Harrington was also a vigorous opponent of the Vietnam War, which put him at odds with much of his socialist brethren, who sought to oppose the spread of Communism.

Finally, we examine how Robert Kennedy's Catholic faith, deepened after his brother's assassination through his reading of the Greek tragedians and Albert Camus, affected his subsequent formulation of public policy. Robert Kennedy was the most religious of the Kennedy brothers; he attended Mass and prayed regularly, said the rosary, went to confession, and read the Bible to his children every night when he was at home. He focused his public work on assisting the poor and minorities, with special attention to the problems facing African Americans, Native Americans and Latinos. He fought against the Vietnam War, seeing it as both immoral and as stripping needed funds away from the poor. He saw welfare as destructive of self-respect, and as an affront to the recipient's human dignity. In its place, Kennedy, like Michael Harrington, called for job creation, advocating a public-private coalition to create jobs, and government to supply them as an employer of last resort. Kennedy opposed the New Deal top-down model of federal direction of poverty programs in favor of local community development initiatives, funded by federal and private monies. In advocating this community-based model, he was aligned with Catholic social justice concepts of decision-making being done at the lowest appropriate level.

CHAPTER SIX

AL SMITH: THE CATHOLIC AS PROGRESSIVE

In 1928, the Democratic Party nominated four-term New York Governor Alfred E. Smith as its presidential candidate. Although favored at the outset of the election, Smith lost in a landslide in which his Republican opponent, Herbert Hoover, took nearly sixty percent of the popular vote. The explanation for this reversal of fortune lay in a complex of factors, including Smith's opposition to Prohibition and his support of immigrants, but a significant causative factor in his loss was Smith's Roman Catholic religion. Moreover, Smith was the champion of urban America, and set the stage for the Democratic Party to gain the vote of that increasingly powerful constituency in future years. But in 1928, the country was not ready for a Catholic, wet president whose idea of Progressive reform was targeted to his urban immigrant supporters, many of whom were Catholic, Jewish, or African-American. While none of his policy positions were ever explicitly tied to Catholic teaching, many of them aligned well with the guiding principles of Catholic social thought, including a respect for the human dignity of each person and the common good, a preferential option for the poor, and subsidiarity – the concept that action should be taken by the lowest grouping (such as local or state government) competent to deal with the issue, rather than elevating the issue to a higher authority (such as the federal government).

EARLY LIFE

Alfred E. Smith was born in New York City on December 30, 1873. His ancestry was Irish and English on his mother's side, and Italian and German on his father's side. His father, a Civil War veteran, was a teamster, while his mother was a factory worker, and later a grocer.

The Smiths lived on the Lower East Side, which was then a pluralistic immigrant neighborhood which was principally Irish, but had a large population teaming with many other immigrant groups, including Italians, Germans, Scandinavians, and even some Chinese.

Smith received his grammar school education in his local parish school at Saint James Roman Catholic Church. He attended that school to eighth grade, when he was forced to drop out, at the age of fourteen, after his father died, in order to support his family. While at St. James, he won the silver medal in a citywide elocution contest when he was twelve years old.

Smith worked at a variety of menial jobs, most notably as a clerk in the Fulton Fish Market, an experience which he would invoke on a regular basis in his political career, often referring to himself as an "F.F.M. man." Extremely articulate, Smith took up acting and became a talented amateur actor playing many different roles. He capitalized on his acting background in his political career, becoming a powerful speaker and commanding presence on the campaign trail. Possessing an excellent memory which was polished by the need to memorize lines in his acting career, Smith was able in later years to give long extemporaneous speeches based upon an encyclopedic knowledge of the details of state government business.

In 1900, Smith married Catherine Dunn, with whom he had five children. The Smiths had an ideal marriage, and remained close until her death in 1944. From his earliest days, Al Smith loved animals, and surrounded himself, in David Burner's wonderful phrase, "with a disorder of pets." This love of animals accompanied him to the Governor's Mansion in Albany, where he had a zoo populated by a variety of species, including a bear.

POLITICAL CAREER

Smith was taken under the wing of Tom Foley, the local boss of the Tammany Hall political machine, who gave Smith his start in politics. With Tammany Hall backing, Smith won a seat in the New York State Assembly in 1903, and was reelected each year to 1915. His early days in the Assembly were not happy. Smith was challenged by the legislative process, and often was unable to comprehend the details of the legislation on which he voted. He thought of dropping out of the legislature, but was urged by Foley to remain. He did so, and became a serious student of the legislative process, learning the details of each piece of proposed legislation, and mastering the process through careful study. He was always prepared in legislative and political debates, and became fond of saying "let's look at the record," dredging up relevant facts from the depths of the legislative history.

Smith became friends with future United States Senator Robert Wagner, and the two became staunch allies in advocating for social reform and labor legislation. In 1911, Smith was elected Democratic Majority Leader and chair of the powerful State Assembly Ways & Means Committee. He ascended to greater public visibility through his service as vice chair on the Factory Investigating Commission chaired by Wagner, which spent years thoroughly investigating the notorious Triangle Shirtwaist Company fire, in which 146 workers, including children, died on March 25, 1911. The Commission broadened its inquiry from fire safety into an examination of general working conditions and hazards of the workplace. It held extensive hearings lasting over one year, and Smith himself personally visited factories and spent up to three days a week working on the investigation.

Based on his work on the Factory Investigating Commission, Smith led the fight in the State Assembly for several new laws on safety, including 32 proposed bills on subjects such as working conditions, mandatory sprinklers, requirements that doors open to the outside, limits on child labor, protections for women workers, and regulation of the hours of work. While not all of these proposals were enacted, Smith was a major force in securing the adoption of many of them.

In 1913, Smith was elected Speaker of the Assembly, becoming both the first Irish Catholic and the first member of Tammany Hall to hold that position. As was the case throughout his political career, Smith's emphasis was placed upon protecting the urban immigrant population; securing industrial reform; and reordering state government to make it more efficient.

Smith switched from state to city government in 1915, with his election to the position of Sheriff of New York City, a position which paid him a greatly increased salary, which helped him to support his growing family. He became President of the New York City Board of Aldermen in 1917, thereby assuming the second most powerful position in the city government.

GOVERNOR AL SMITH

1918 saw a great change in the trajectory of Al Smith's political career. He was tapped by Tammany Hall to run for Governor as the Democratic nominee, a nomination also desired by the newspaper publisher, William Randolph Hearst, whom Tammany did not trust. Hearst, whose life was fictionalized as "Citizen Kane" in the Orson Wells movie, also unsuccessfully sought the Democratic nomination against Smith in 1922.

Smith would serve four terms as New York's governor. He won in 1918 by a narrow margin of about 15,000 votes. Smith's victory was delivered by Manhattan and Brooklyn, which gave him a lead of 186,000, with Smith winning 80 percent of the Irish vote and over 70 percent of the Italian and German vote. He lost for reelection in 1920, in the Republican landslide nationally, which saw Warren Harding elected president.

Smith won again in the gubernatorial elections of 1922, 1924, and 1926, with a margin of 250,000 votes in his last victory. His base continued to be among urban ethnic immigrants, with great majorities among Irish, Italian, and Jewish voters. The alliance of immigrant Catholics and Jews, which came to characterize New York politics, was especially powerful under Smith, whose three chief advisers were all Jewish.

Smith's principal adviser was Judge Joseph Proskauer, who grew up in Alabama, but came north to attend Columbia College and stayed on in the city to go to Columbia Law School. Proskauer was appointed to the trial bench in New York in 1923 by Smith, and then promoted by him in 1927 to the appellate bench. After Smith's loss to Herbert Hoover in the 1928 presidential election, Proskauer began what became a nationally prominent law firm in 1930, where he was the senior partner until he died in 1971. His Catholic ties persisted after Smith's death, when Proskauer helped in the drafting of *Nostra Aetate*, the Vatican II Declaration on Catholic relations with other religious traditions.

A second adviser was Belle Moskowitz, a brilliant strategist who helped Smith win support from newly enfranchised women voters. Moskowitz also had close ties with the African-American community, and her husband, Henry, had been one of the founders of the NAACP. Smith's third principal adviser was Robert Moses, who would become the famous city planner and adviser to a succession of New York governors. All three of these advisers also became close friends with Smith.

This Catholic-Jewish alliance endangered Smith's national political ambitions because this was the era of dominance of the second Ku Klux Klan, which reorganized in 1915, aiming now not just at African-Americans, but even more viciously at Catholics and Jews. The Klan was a national force, with strength in the North as well as in the South. Indeed, its largest number of members in any state was in Indiana. It reached an apex of over four million in membership nationally in 1924, when Smith sought the Democratic presidential nomination.

Smith's policies emerged clearly in his first term, when he fought for both civil liberties and the interests of his urban immigrant supporters. He opposed the ouster from the state legislature of five Socialists who had been duly elected, but who were opposed as subversives following the "red scares" of the post World War I period. In support of civil liberties, he also vetoed bills setting up a state police agency aimed at indicting radicals; prescribing loyalty tests for teachers; and empowering courts to strike subversive parties from the ballot. To protect the urban immigrant, he vetoed bills increasing classes on American values for factory workers and immigrants, and requiring that state licensing of private schools take into account the school's record in advancing American values. Smith also became famous for reorganizing state government to make its administration of public money less costly and more efficient.

Smith's record as four-term governor was in line with the nobler part of the legacy of the Progressive Movement of the times. He fought for administrative and social reform and protective legislation, including increased funding for education and public health, increased inspections of factories, additional safety legislation, expansion of parks and conservation, and more and better housing, as well as for civil liberties for all. Significantly, however, unlike many other Progressives, he opposed the Klan and its pet projects of immigration restrictions and Prohibition, which he rightly perceived as being unfairly aimed at his urban immigrant constituency. These stands, along with his Roman Catholic religion, led to his political martyrdom when he entered the stage of national politics, seeking the Democratic Party's nomination for President of the United States.

PRESIDENTIAL CAMPAIGNS

Al Smith was nominated for president four times. This process began in 1920, when his name was first placed in nomination at the Democratic Convention. This was not a serious effort at obtaining the nomination, but rather an introduction of Smith to a wider, national audience. When Smith's name was placed in nomination, the Tammany Hall band played a number of New York themed songs, including most memorably "The Sidewalks of New York."

Smith made his first major effort at obtaining the Democratic Party's presidential nomination in 1924. His nomination speech was delivered by Franklin D. Roosevelt, who introduced Smith as "the happy warrior." That memorable phrase was coined by Joseph Proskauer, but Roosevelt had resisted using both it and the speech that Proskauer had prepared. Smith battled with William Gibbs McAdoo for the nomination. McAdoo was Woodrow Wilson's son-in-law and a former Secretary of the Treasury. He was also perceived as being the favored son of the Ku Klux Klan. When neither Smith nor McAdoo was able to win enough ballots, the convention turned to Wall Street lawyer John W. Davis as a compromise nominee after some 103 ballots had been taken.

The 1924 Democratic Convention made it evident that defeating Smith was a major national priority for the Ku Klux Klan, which referred to him not as "the happy warrior," but rather as "the pope-loving governor of '*Jew* York.'"

Smith was nominated again in 1928 by Roosevelt at the Democratic Convention held in Houston, Texas. This time he secured the nomination over the bitter opposition of the Klan and southern states. Opposition to Smith's candidacy rested in part on his urban immigrant background and his well-known opposition to Prohibition, but much of it was fueled by virulent anti-Catholicism along the lines of that we saw above in the Prologue. Indeed, statistical analysis of the 1928 vote strongly suggests that religion provided the best explanation for the opposition to Smith in that election. Smith's opposition to Prohibition and identification with immigrants only served to aggravate the anti-Catholicism of Protestants, since many denominations, led by the Methodists and Baptists, supported Prohibition, with an aim to controlling both immigrants and blacks.

The opposition of the Ku Klux Klan to Smith was incredibly hostile. The Klan began that opposition early, with a march on Washington D. C. in 1925, protesting the near nomination of Smith at the 1924 Democratic Convention. The march was the largest ever held in Washington to that date, with some 500,000 people participating. The Klan's opposition to Smith was supported in more rational terms by other commentators. Particularly noteworthy was an open letter by lawyer Charles C. Marshall which was published in the April 1927 issue of the *Atlantic Monthly*. Marshall was an expert on canon law, and utilized excerpts from papal encyclicals to argue his position that Smith's Catholic religion was incompatible with both the United States Constitution and American values.

Smith's response, entitled "Catholic and Patriot: Governor Smith Replies," was printed in the May 1927 issue of the *Atlantic Monthly*. Written by Joseph Proskauer, with assistance on Catholic doctrine provided by the famous World War I chaplain, Father Francis Duffy, the article took the same approach that John F. Kennedy would later follow in the 1960 presidential campaign. Smith declared his support for separation of church and state, and pledged not to permit his religious beliefs to interfere with the performance of his constitutional duties.

The 1928 national presidential campaign was remarkable for its anti-Catholic rhetoric. In his excellent biography of Smith, Robert Slayton devotes an entire chapter, which he titles "And the Pope Will Move to Washington," to this rhetoric. Here are just a few examples:

Tom Heflin, a United States senator from and Alabama, declared that "The Roman Catholic edict has gone forth in secret articles, 'Al Smith is to be made President'...They will lay the heavy hand of a Catholic state upon you and crush the life out of Protestantism in America." He also promised that the "the Protestants of America are determined to keep Popery out of the White House."

A group of Protestant ministers from Atlanta, Georgia, protested that the "You cannot nail us to a Roman cross and submerge us in a sea of rum"

A headline in *The American Standard* reported that "Rome suggests That Pope May Move Here."

In Daytona Beach, Florida, the local school board gave children cards to take home to their parents. The cards read that if Al Smith were elected, "you will not be allowed to have or read a Bible."

The mainline Protestant publication, *the Christian Century*, joined the chorus of these less elevated publications, stating its opposition to Smith because he was "a representative of an alien culture, of a medieval Latin mentality, of an undemocratic hierarchy and of a foreign potentate." It concluded that there was "a real issue between Catholicism and American institutions."

Newspapers and magazines produced a flurry of cartoons opposing Smith because of his Catholic religion. One of the most highly reproduced cartoons pictures Smith as kneeling and kissing a cleric's ring, under the caption "and he asks the American people to elect him President!"

In a campaign address delivered in Oklahoma City in September of 1928, Smith challenged the flurry of anti- Catholic articles, one of which suggested that "the church had purchased high ground on which artillery could be trained on the federal government." Smith pointed to "The constitutional guaranty that there should be no religious test for office." He added that "The absolute separation of State and Church is part of the fundamental basis of our Constitution. I believe in that separation, and in all that it implies." He also attacked the Ku Klux Klan in the same speech, pointing out that "There is no greater mockery in this world today than the burning of the Cross... by these people who are spreading this propaganda... while the Christ that they are supposed to adore, love and venerate ... taught the holy, sacred writ of brotherly love."

Smith's efforts to defuse the attacks on his religion failed. He lost the presidential election to the Republican candidate, Herbert Hoover. Hoover soundly defeated Smith, taking 58 percent of the popular vote. Smith carried only eight states, but won the combined vote of the nation's twelve largest cities. This was the first time a Democratic candidate had done so, and began the ascendancy of the Democratic Party in national politics among urban dwellers.

SMITH'S CAREER AFTER POLITICS

For all practical purposes, Smith's political career ended in the debacle of the 1928 presidential election. Nevertheless, he attempted to run for president once more in 1932. While he defeated his old ally, Franklin D. Roosevelt, in several early primaries, he lost the nomination to Roosevelt on the fourth ballot.

Smith began a business career after the 1928 election, and became president of the Empire State Building Corporation, as well as a board member of several corporations. His financial situation worsened, however, with the stock market crash in 1929. In addition, the resulting Great Depression left the Empire State Building with a majority of unleased space. Smith turned to writing articles and books, including an autobiography, to make ends meet.

After Roosevelt's election as president in 1932, Smith began to oppose the New Deal, concluding that it was socialistic and that Roosevelt was becoming a demagogue. Even before Roosevelt was inaugurated, Smith told the Democratic Jefferson Day Dinner that "I will take off my coat and fight to the end against any candidate who persists in any demagogic appeal to the masses of the working people of this country to destroy themselves by setting class against class and rich against poor." When President Roosevelt decided to abandon the gold standard, Smith opposed him, charging that the change led to "baloney dollars." Smith also believed that Roosevelt got off track by seeking solutions to the country's financial crisis at the federal level, rather than recognizing the primacy of state government to address such problems.

In the two succeeding presidential elections, Smith supported the Republican candidates – Alf Landon in 1936 and Wendell Willkie in 1940. While at least some portion of his opposition to Roosevelt can be traced to bitter feelings from his experience in 1932 Democratic Convention, Smith also felt that Roosevelt was not up to the job and was pursuing socialistic solutions to the country's problems.

In his later years, Smith continued to speak up for persecuted minorities both here and abroad. In 1933, he became the first significant public figure in the United States to speak publicly against Adolf Hitler's persecution of the Jews in Germany. He also denounced white racism in a 1941 speech at Lincoln University, a largely African-American institution, and had had a long experience of working with black leaders from his Tammany Hall days.

In retirement, Smith's many contributions to the public good went largely unrecognized except by the Catholic Church, which made him a Knight of Malta and a Papal Chamberlain. Notre Dame University also awarded him the prestigious Laetare Medal.

Al Smith died in October 1944, shortly after the death of his beloved wife in May of that year. His funeral filled St. Patrick's Cathedral to overflowing, and 200,000 people went past his coffin, which was allowed to lie in state at the cathedral the night before his funeral mass.

Smith's Catholicism

Catholicism was a major influence in Al Smith's formation. He attended Catholic grammar school, served as an altar boy, and saw priests as both mentors and friends. Throughout his life, he attended Mass regularly. Smith's daughter told an interviewer that the Catholic Church was "the heart and center of the parish," and "an intimate part of our daily lives."

Smith was not educated on the finer points of Catholic doctrine, and admitted that he was not familiar with the details of papal encyclicals or other pronouncements by the Vatican. Nevertheless, his positions on public issues aligned with the general principles of Catholic social thought, including respect for the human dignity of every individual, concern for the common good, and devotion to the interests of immigrants and the urban poor.

While Smith rarely invoked Catholic teachings in his public life, there are some traces of the impact of church teachings on him. For example, during the hearings on the Triangle Shirtwaist Fire, Smith supported the comment by another member of the commission that those who died were "human souls," and not just statistics. Smith observed that the comment reflected "good Catholic doctrine." Smith also argued, during the same hearings, for the enactment of legislation which would limit the work week to six days. Those who opposed such legislation, Smith observed, would "rewrite the Divine law" to read "Remember the Sabbath day, to keep it holy — except in the canneries." Finally, his sense of the proper division of power between state and federal government was consistent with the doctrine of Catholic social thought known as subsidiarity. Under this doctrine, decisions affecting the lives of people should properly be made at the lowest competent level. Smith's substantive opposition to Franklin Roosevelt's New Deal was consistent with this philosophy, because it was based in part on his belief that Roosevelt improperly imposed federal solutions on problems that were more appropriately addressed at the state level.

AL SMITH: THE CATHOLIC AS PROGRESSIVE

Historians today see the Progressive Movement as flawed because of its anti-immigrant and anti-African-American biases, which are manifested in support for such policies as eugenics, restrictions on immigration, compulsory public school attendance, segregation, and Prohibition. These policies were rooted in the belief that enlightened "experts" could impose from above structure and order on an increasingly diverse society. Segregation and Prohibition, for example, were seen as ways to control, protect, and isolate African-Americans and immigrants, while the Progressive transformation of white, Anglo-Saxon society went about its reforms.

Smith's positions, from his days in the city at Tammany Hall throughout his presidential campaigns, embraced and advanced the best of the Progressive Movement, while opposing these perverted strains of "reform." Smith chose instead to support social reform legislation of the type which protected laborers and consumers, while at the same time zealously safeguarding the civil liberties of every individual, even those who were despised by the reformers, including Socialists, immigrants, African-Americans, Catholics and Jews. While this was a Progressivism that most would support today, it was not a platform the electorate of 1928 was prepared to endorse.

CHAPTER SEVEN

MICHAEL HARRINGTON: THE CATHOLIC AS SOCIALIST

"The equal dignity of human persons requires the effort to reduce excessive social and economic inequalities. It gives urgency to the elimination of sinful inequalities."

"[T]hose who are oppressed by poverty are the object of a *preferential love* on the part of the Church which, since her origin and in spite of the failings of many of her members, has not ceased to work for their relief, defense, and liberation through numerous works of charity which remain indispensible always and everywhere."

The Catechism of the Catholic Church (1994)

Virtually all of the individuals we have discussed so far have been practicing Catholics. That is not the case with Michael Harrington who, although born and raised Catholic, became an atheist while he was still in his twenties. Nevertheless, as Harrington himself often acknowledged, his adopted socialism was heavily influenced and tempered by his Catholicism. Harrington's personal journey reflects a comment made by Pete Hamill: "Even for those Catholics who do not practice anymore, who have lost religious faith, there are also many ways to be Catholic. The actor Peter O'Toole once said to me: 'There is no such thing as an ex-Catholic. But there are many retired Catholics'." Michael Harrington belonged to that club.

EARLY LIFE AND EDUCATION

Edward Michael Harrington was born in St. Louis, Missouri, on February 24, 1928. He was the only child of Edward Michael

Harrington, Senior, and Catherine Harrington. His father was a lawyer who eventually specialized in patent law, while his mother was active in volunteer work and had a master's degree in Economics from St. Louis University. The Harringtons provided their son with sixteen years of Catholic education, including high school at St. Louis University High School, a Jesuit institution, followed by an undergraduate education at the College of the Holy Cross in Massachusetts, another Jesuit institution.

Following his graduation from Holy Cross, Harrington went on to attend one year of law school at Yale University. Although he did well academically at Yale, making the law review based on his grades, he dropped out after one year. His next academic stop was at the University of Chicago, where he received a master's degree in English Literature. At that point, he planned to become a poet, but instead became a volunteer at Dorothy Day's Catholic Worker in New York.

EARLY WRITING, SOCIAL WORK, AND POLITICAL INVOLVEMENT

When Michael Harrington started at the Catholic Worker in 1951, the volunteers would tell people that they came to the Catholic Worker because they wanted to be saints. Harrington was struggling with his Catholic faith at the time, and saw Dorothy Day's group as being "as far Left as you could go within the Church." He took a voluntary oath of poverty, read a breviary, and attended Mass and received communion on a regular basis. Ultimately, however, as we discuss below, Harrington left the Church permanently at the end of 1952.

Harrington's time at the Catholic Worker focused more on writing and speaking, than on one-to-one service to the poor. He became one of the three editors at the Catholic Worker's newspaper, where he wrote reviews and essays on a wide variety of books in philosophy and religion, and occasionally on fiction as well. Harrington came to believe that the orientation of the group favoring a rural lifestyle was wrong, and that the Catholic Worker was too arrogant and self-righteous, and was not actually serving the real interests of the poor. In his view, the organization concentrated too much on saving individuals, ignoring the institutional mechanisms which contributed to poverty, and which had to be changed to address the underlying problem.

During his time at the Catholic Worker, Harrington made several key contacts which would serve to advance his public profile for the rest of his life. For example, he met William F. Buckley, the noted conservative who had been an undergraduate at Yale while Harrington attended law school at that institution. Harrington debated Buckley on several occasions and continued to do so over the years, appearing several times on Buckley's television program, "Firing Line." Harrington also met and became friendly with John Cogley, the executive editor of *Commonweal* Magazine. Harrington became a regular contributor to that lay Catholic publication, writing nearly fifty book reviews, articles and essays for the magazine over the years. Cogley also hired Harrington to work on a 1956 study done by the Fund for the Republic, which critically examined the blacklisting of suspected communists and other radicals by Hollywood in the McCarthy era. During his time at the Catholic Worker, Harrington also became friendly with the radical editor and writer, Dwight MacDonald.

At the end of 1952, Harrington left the Catholic Worker to become the executive secretary of the Workers Defense League, a left-wing legal advocacy group. He also began to spend more of his time developing a career as a writer for left-wing and liberal publications. These included Irving Howe's *Dissent*, for which he began writing in 1955, and both the *Village Voice* and *Commentary*. He became an editor of *Dissent* in 1957. These vehicles were critical in developing Harrington's reputation, and his influence in left-wing politics stemmed mainly from his writing and speaking ability, enhanced by a charismatic personality.

HARRINGTON'S POLITICS

After he left the Catholic Worker in 1952, Harrington's career became associated with the various groups allied with the largely moribund Socialist Party in the United States. He told acquaintances in later years that he had become converted to socialism in his one year stay at Yale Law School, where many of his prior, conservative Catholic ideas had been challenged by other, more radical students. Harrington's socialism became an embarrassment to some of his sponsors, including John Cogley. Cogley was called before the House of Representatives' Un-American Activities Committee in 1956, and was questioned in his appearance, among other things, on whether he was aware that Harrington was a socialist when he hired him as an assistant on the Fund for the Republic study on Hollywood blacklisting.

Over the years, Harrington jumped from one small group to another in the highly contentious and fragmented world of socialist splinter organizations. There is consistency in his movements, as Harrington joined those groups which opposed Communism, and were open to working with the Democratic Party to create a realigned political organization of liberals.

In 1968, Harrington was elected chairman of the Socialist Party in the United States, after it had been taken over by a conservative, anti-communist group. He resigned as chairman when the controlling faction refused actively to support George McGovern, the Democratic Party's 1972 presidential nominee because of McGovern's opposition to the Vietnam War.

Harrington started a new group in 1973, which was christened the Democratic Socialist Organizing Committee. In Harrington's view, the organization was to be "democratic, humanist, and antiwar." The DSOC merged in 1982 with the New American Movement, another splinter group which favored community activism, and the merged group worked with Democrats to unite labor, civil rights activists, women, and liberals.

With the emergence of new socialist and other New Left groups in the 1970s, Harrington lost influence, and remained a socialist as part of what he termed a Pascalian wager. By that time, he saw socialism as "still beginning, a task to be accomplished, not a destiny to be awaited." He also remained a Marxist, but one who was committed to participatory democracy. Harrington saw his role as one of updating the classic Marxist framework to advance democracy and address the new problems posed by the emergence of bureaucracies.

THE OTHER AMERICA

While Harrington wrote nineteen books on topics ranging from socialism and capitalism to politics and poverty, including three which were autobiographical, his reputation rests primarily on his

1962 book, *The Other America*. That book sold 70,000 copies in the first year after publication, and over one million through today. *Time* Magazine selected it as one of the ten most influential nonfiction books of the twentieth century.

In 1962, the popular intellectual focus was on the problems of the affluent society, and the poor were not high on the radar screen of the public intellectuals. Harrington changed that. In his book, building on work he had done previously in *Commentary* Magazine, Harrington wrote a high-level overview of the many faces of poverty, arguing that poverty was "a culture, an institution, a way of life." (*The Other America*, 16) He argued that, unlike the prior poverty of ethnic immigrants from Europe, "the new poverty is constructed so as to destroy aspiration; it is a system designed to be impervious to hope." (10) By contrast, the old ethnic neighborhoods of big cities had "a lusty richness of existence," which fostered both community and aspiration. (141)

Harrington estimated that some forty to fifty million people - up to twenty-five percent of all Americans - lived in poverty. These people include minorities, the elderly poor, the unemployed, unskilled workers, migrant farm workers, small farmers, those living in urban slums and poor rural areas like Appalachia, alcoholics, and even poor bohemian intellectuals. To this long list must be added the children of each of these families. The genius of *The Other America* lies in Harrington's demonstration that the poor, although they are often hidden from general view, include all races, and populate all parts of America ranging from small rural farms to the slums of the large cities, and are not confined to urban ghettos.

Harrington examined the particular problems of each of these groups separately. In one chapter, for example, he documented the lives of the two million migrant workers who included "Anglos," African-Americans and Mexicans whom he described as being on a "pilgrimage of misery" performing "work that is too delicate for machines and to dirty for any but the dispossessed." (40) In another chapter, he illustrates the different problems experienced by the eight million poor elderly persons needing medical and housing assistance. He also devotes a chapter to documenting through statistics both the increased incidence and severity of mental illness among the

American poor, showing a general failure to treat mental illness in this population.

Harrington's socialist beliefs are never explicitly stated in the book, but his view of labor as a savior does in several places. He characterizes labor as the most powerful force speaking for the poor in America, seeing organized labor as a "chief avenue of hope" in that "many union legislative proposals — to extend the coverage of minimum wage and social security, to organize migrant farm laborers — articulate the needs of the poor." (6, 59, 173) Harrington closes *The Other America* with a call for "a restructuring of the party system so that there can be clear choices, a new mood of social idealism." (174)

The Other America demonstrates Harrington's strengths as a writer and public intellectual. His writing is direct and engaging, and relatively easy to follow. He employs short, crisp sentences containing few polysyllabic words, and continuously provides word pictures to illustrate his points. The distinctive dress of migrant workers in California, for example, is captured in the sentence "The field hands wear their calling like a skin." (49) The book maintains the reader's interest through the use of multiple vignettes depicting the sorry lives of the poor, interspersed with quotations from poets, playwrights, novelists, and songwriters ranging from William Butler Yeats to Woody Guthrie. Relevant statistics also flow throughout the text and an appendix, lending the book an authoritative air.

The Other America came to the attention of President John F. Kennedy, who asked his staff to develop an anti-poverty program. That program was implemented after his assassination by his successor, Lyndon Baines Johnson, who called it the "War on Poverty." President Johnson appointed Kennedy's brother-in-law Sargent Shriver to head the program, and Shriver enlisted Harrington to serve as a member of the War on Poverty Task Force for a brief period of weeks.

Harrington proposed a "vast and comprehensive program attacking the culture of poverty" to be planned and carried out at the federal level. (166) His approach called for providing more jobs through New Deal type public works programs. Johnson rejected this approach, not wishing to spend the billions of dollars required to implement such programs. He preferred instead to establish job training programs and similar self-help approaches.

Harrington also proposed to address the problems of the eight million elderly poor who were unable to work through an expansion of the welfare state, providing more, cheaper, and earlier medical care, as well as specialized housing for the infirm elderly. (118-119) He also argued that comprehensive medical care should be made available to all Americans. Finally, Harrington proposed a large increase in the building of public housing units, to be scattered among existing neighborhoods, to consist of small buildings with no more than eight families, and not to be confined to current ghetto areas. To facilitate the transition of the poor to these better neighborhoods, he called for the increased availability of social workers. (155-156)

While Harrington's book received widespread attention, his proposals were generally rejected at the time. Subsequently, moreover, the emerging neoconservative movement attacked the underlying premises of the War on Poverty, arguing that the culture of poverty was exacerbated, rather than assisted, by increased government spending. This view contended that government "handouts" made the poor too dependent on government, and sapped their self-reliance. Harrington challenged the neoconservative thesis in a 1973 article in *Dissent*. He argued that the federal government actually spent more money on the middle class, through programs such as Medicare and Social Security, than it did on the poor, whose programs were, in his view, consistently underfunded. Harrington also continued to see full employment as the principal remedy for the poor, as well as for other workers who found themselves unemployed.

HARRINGTON'S POLITICAL PHILOSOPHY

Throughout his political career, Harrington encouraged Socialists to join with Democrats in pursuing structural reforms which would make the country more democratic, and which were politically feasible to attain. His goal, as he had called for in *The Other America*, was to facilitate a political realignment which would make the Democratic Party a vehicle of reform for American society. He was joined in this goal by labor leaders such as Walter Reuther, head of the United Auto Workers. Harrington visualized the emergence of a new liberal party which would combine union members, the poor, and African-Americans with a new "conscience constituency" of middle class college graduates who worked in the professions or in the new technology sector.

Harrington's goal was not shared by members of the emerging New Left. They opposed attempts to cooperate with the existing political system, which they saw as corrupt. In their eyes, even the War on Poverty was a fraud, and the entire system needed to be overthrown.

Beginning in the 1950s, Harrington worked with African-American leaders to incorporate black Americans into his new coalition. Based upon his prior friendship with Bayard Rustin, Harrington worked along with other black leaders, including Martin Luther King Jr., to obtain a strong civil rights plank at the 1960 Democratic Convention. He continued his work with King in the later 1960s by joining King's informal research committee, and pursued efforts to include African-Americans in a realigned, liberal Democratic Party.

Harrington also opposed the Vietnam War, a position which divided him from certain elements of the socialist movement which supported the war because of an uncompromising opposition to Communism and its expansion. In a newspaper article in the *New York Herald Tribune*, Harrington explained that his opposition to the war was based upon a belief that "the fate of Appalachia may well be determined in the jungles of Viet Nam." His opposition to the war antagonized the New Left, as did Harrington's criticism of their naïve embrace of Ho Chi Minh and the Viet Cong.

Harrington consistently participated in the mainstream political process by seeking to advance the candidacies of liberals for the Democratic presidential nomination. In 1968, he first supported the anti-war candidacy of Senator Eugene McCarthy of Minnesota against President Lyndon Johnson, but switched to Senator Robert Kennedy of New York when Kennedy entered the race. Harrington was a political pragmatist, and he believed that Kennedy had a better chance of uniting workers with the poor, and the middle class conscience constituency with radicals, than did the cerebral and often abrasive McCarthy. Harrington campaigned for Kennedy, and was on the funeral train with Kennedy's body following Kennedy's assassination after his victory in the California Democratic presidential primary. After Kennedy's death, Harrington turned back to McCarthy and supported his unsuccessful candidacy for the 1968 nomination.

In 1972, Harrington originally threw his support to Senator Edmund Muskie of Maine. Muskie, like McCarthy and Kennedy, was a Roman Catholic. When Muskie's candidacy faltered, Harrington turned to support the eventual nominee, Senator George McGovern of South Dakota. In 1976, Harrington initially supported Congressman Morris Udall of Arizona for the Democratic presidential nomination, but once again agreed to support the eventual ticket of Jimmy Carter and Walter Mondale based upon a strong liberal platform which came out of the Democratic Convention. That platform called for both national health insurance and legislation supporting full employment.

By 1980, Harrington had become disillusioned with President Carter because of his inability to advance liberal initiatives. In that year he supported Senator Edward Kennedy of Massachusetts (another Catholic) in his unsuccessful bid to wrest the nomination from Carter, and did not endorse Carter in the presidential campaign of that year, in which Ronald Reagan emerged victorious.

Harrington continued his support of liberals for the Democratic presidential nomination in both 1984 and 1988, the year before he died. In 1984, he was particularly enthusiastic for the candidacy of Walter Mondale, and saw Mondale's campaign as uniting "all of the class and social forces we had deemed essential." Finally, in 1988, Harrington supported the candidacy of Reverend Jesse Jackson, whose Rainbow Coalition embodied the political realignment Harrington had so long sought.

In continuing his lifelong outreach to students, Harrington began teaching at Queens College of the City University of New York in 1972. He began as a lecturer in political science, and eventually was named Distinguished Professor of Political Science at that institution in 1988. He died of cancer in July of the following year.

HARRINGTON'S RELIGIOUS JOURNEY

In 1978, Michael Harrington told the *Christian Century* that "I am a pious apostate, an atheist shocked by the faithlessness of believers, a fellow traveler of moderate Catholicism who has been out of the church for 20 years." That "moderate Catholicism" helped to form his social conscience, and continued to inform his policy positions over the years, even as his faith in the religion ultimately failed.

Harrington began his life as a traditional Catholic of the post World War II period. When he graduated from the College of the Holy

Cross, for example, he was chosen to give the Salutatory Address, and his speech emphasized that every person "has a moral worth and dignity," and is created in the "image of God," both of which are core concepts of the Catholic faith.

When he got to Yale Law School, he began to doubt his faith. This was the era of Legal Realism where the natural law concepts Harrington had learned throughout his Catholic education were attacked as naïve, and the previously skilled debater found himself unable to convince his fellow law students that his religious beliefs were valid. The doubt which began at Yale grew at the University of Chicago. Harrington found himself doubting the reality of a God who would send people to hell and concluded that the whole "Jesuit house of cards" had collapsed. At that point, Harrington concluded that he would leave the Catholic faith in favor of an "indecisive apostasy." In 1950, he told the priest who chaired the philosophy department at Saint Louis University that he had left the church.

By the next year, however, his indecisiveness continued, and he returned to the Catholic faith after reading the works of Blaise Pascal and Soren Kierkegaard. Borrowing from Pascal, he concluded that he would make a wager that God existed, and consequently began attending Mass, receiving communion, and reading a breviary during his days at the Catholic Worker in 1951 and 1952.

His Pascalian wager ended in December of 1952, when he left the Catholic Church for good. He wrote that he "no longer believed in the faith, not even by way of an existential leap." His decision severely distressed his family, and when he married a Jewish journalist, Stephanie Gervis in 1963, his mother did not attend the wedding in Paris, France.

Despite Harrington's abandonment of the Catholic faith, it continued to influence him. Indeed, as Harrington continued to acknowledge for the rest of his life, the Catholic faith he grew up in helped him to formulate his political and social philosophy. In the Acknowledgements section at the beginning of *The Other America*, Harrington began by noting that "It was through Dorothy Day and the Catholic Worker movement that I first came into contact with the terrible reality of involuntary poverty and the magnificent ideal of voluntary poverty." Harrington also relied upon Catholic social teaching in the years after he left the Church. One example of this comes from his opposition to the use of atomic weapons by any party or state, relying on the Catholic just war theory. In taking this stand, Harrington opposed those hard-line socialists who reasoned that the use of atomic weapons could be justified if it advanced the socialist cause.

Harrington also believed that morality had to be incorporated into politics, and praised Albert Camus' *The Rebel* in a 1954 review for advocating this position. Harrington was also impressed with the papacy of Pope John XXIII, particularly in his encyclicals covering issues of social justice and peace. He perceived the reforms of Vatican II as moving the Catholic Church away from its former preoccupation with Communism and towards broader issues of social justice.

MICHAEL HARRINGTON: CATHOLIC SOCIALIST

Michael Harrington's journey to socialism started on the road of Catholicism. Like many liberal Catholics today, he chose to embrace the more radical side of the religion, in its teachings on social justice. Indeed, while the Catholic Church has consistently opposed socialism, the substance of Harrington's program of socialist politics was consistent with that set forth by Monsignor John Ryan in the 1919 *Bishops Program of Social Reconstruction*, which we discussed in the Prologue. Remember also that Franklin Delano Roosevelt, as president, pointed out that the Catholic Church's encyclicals on the rights of labor were more radical than the proposals he set forth in his New Deal. While Harrington may have abandoned the faith of his fathers, he continued to champion the faith's more radical views on how society should be reconstructed.

CHAPTER EIGHT

ROBERT F. KENNEDY: THE CATHOLIC AS PEOPLES' TRIBUNE

"Seeing the photographs and footage of him in clapboard shacks, with those endlessly sad eyes, bending to speak to children in rags, I always thought of Christ's words: 'If you did it for the least of my brethren, you did it for me...He was the best sort of Catholic. There was no lip service to his religion. He was living it as surely, often more surely, than any priest."

Anna Quindlen

A FUNERAL TRAIN

Robert Kennedy was forty two years old when he died from an assassin's bullets one day after he won the California Democratic presidential primary. While the opposition to Kennedy's candidacy had been uncommonly fierce, the deep sadness which flowed over the poor people of the country after his assassination leaps from the pictures taken of the crowds standing, kneeling, and sitting along the tracks traveled by his funeral train on June 8, 1968. Estimates put their number between one and two million.

As the train traveled from Pennsylvania Station in New York to Union Station in Washington D.C., the people along the tracks included all races and social classes, but the poor and minorities clearly predominated. White policemen could be seen holding up black children so that they could see the train better. At one point, black militants held up their clenched fists in a salute to Kennedy while, at another, white workingmen held up American flags as their tribute to him. There was even the unique scene of a bridal party in

Delaware whose bridesmaids threw their bouquets at the train as it passed by.

Photographer Paul Fusco captured the individualized faces of palpable grief, white and black, young and old, male and female, along the tracks. One of his pictures shows a white man standing on the tracks looking for the train. He is dressed in stained pants and a sleeveless undershirt which is also deeply stained, with a hole in it. He wears a look of anger. Behind him a young boy in glasses (his son, perhaps) holds his hand over his heart while his older sister, near tears, clasps his hand, and enfolds her other hand with that of an older female relative. All appear to be poor. Further down the same track, black people stand side-by-side with whites. Virtually all, white and black, appear stunned. These are not the faces of curiosity; they are the faces of those who have lost a family member.

A nurse who took her family to the train tracks told her children that Robert Kennedy was "someone way up there who hadn't forgotten the rest of us way down here and wanted the country to get better and better."

Arthur Schlesinger, Jr., the Kennedy house historian, recorded this aspect of Robert Kennedy's appeal in a chapter heading in his lengthy biography of Kennedy, calling him the "Tribune of the Underclass." The poet Robert Lowell captured the same thought in verse:

"For them like a prince, you daily left your tower
to walk through dirt in your best cloth."

Robert Kennedy's popularity among the poor and minorities is borne out by the results of the 1968 Democratic presidential primaries. In California, for example, his victory of less than five percent over Senator Eugene McCarthy resulted from majorities of seventy percent among low-income voters, seventy five percent among blacks, and nearly ninety percent among Mexican Americans.

EARLY LIFE AND EDUCATION

Robert Francis Kennedy was born on November 20, 1925. He was the seventh of the nine children of Joseph and Rose Kennedy. His early education included a brief stay at the Episcopal St. Paul's

School in New Hampshire from which he transferred to the Catholic Portsmouth Priory in Rhode Island. He completed his high school education at Milton Academy, a secular school which was a feeder school for Harvard College. Kennedy attended Harvard, where he compiled an undistinguished undergraduate academic record. He did, however, accomplish something none of his larger and stronger brothers was able to do when he attained a varsity letter in football.

Kennedy's academic record at Harvard disqualified him from admission to Harvard Law School. Instead, he attended the University of Virginia Law School in Charlottesville, Virginia, from which he graduated in 1951.

Robert Kennedy's Political Career

Robert Kennedy's political career began early, when he was still in his mid-twenties. In 1952, the year after he graduated from law school, he helped to manage his brother John's campaign for the United States Senate. After that, he joined the notorious Permanent Investigations Committee, which was chaired by Senator Joseph McCarthy of Wisconsin. Kennedy later explained his decision to join McCarthy as having been rooted in his belief that there was a serious threat posed to the internal security of the country from Communism and that only McCarthy was doing something about it. To that explanation he added, "I was wrong." He briefly resigned from the committee in 1953 to work with his father as a staff assistant on the Hoover Commission on Reorganization of the Executive Branch, where he learned firsthand of the inefficiency of the governmental bureaucracy.

In 1954, Kennedy rejoined the Permanent Investigations Committee as minority counsel and steered the committee toward a new focus on organized crime. This ultimately led to intensive public hearings which were widely covered by the media investigating corruption in American labor unions. Kennedy's blistering and sarcastic cross examination of witnesses, combined with his colorful tongue lashings of organized crime figures and labor union officials who invoked the constitutional right against self-incrimination provided by the Fifth Amendment, created a public image of Kennedy as ruthless and ambitious. He never escaped from this early classification by the media, labor officials, and political opponents.

Jack Newfield, a journalist who covered Kennedy's 1968 presidential campaign and became a friend, saw Kennedy differently. While acknowledging that Kennedy was primarily a politician, he added that he also was part "soldier, priest, radical, and football coach."

Robert Kennedy resigned in 1959 from the Permanent Investigations Committee, turning next to work for John F. Kennedy in the presidential campaign of 1960. His brother appointed him Attorney General of the United States, a position in which Robert Kennedy served until 1964. After John F. Kennedy's assassination in November of 1963, a morose Robert Kennedy decided to run for a United States Senate seat from New York. He was elected after a bitter campaign in 1964, and served as a United States senator from 1965 through his death in 1968.

After the escalation of the Vietnam War in 1968 under President Lyndon B. Johnson, and Johnson's close victory over Senator Eugene McCarthy of Minnesota in the Democratic presidential primary in New Hampshire, Robert Kennedy announced his candidacy for President of the United States on March 16, 1968. Between March 16 and June 5, he was victorious in four Democratic presidential primaries, winning Indiana, Nebraska, North Dakota, and California. He lost to McCarthy only in Oregon.

Robert Kennedy was assassinated on the same night he won the California primary, as he left the stage after making his victory speech. He was shot by a Palestinian zealot who fired eight bullets, hitting Kennedy with three, including the headshot that killed him.

ROBERT KENNEDY'S RELIGION

Kennedy began his education at St. Paul's School in New Hampshire. St. Paul's was an Episcopalian school, and the young Robert soon complained to his highly religious Catholic mother, Rose, that he was being subjected to Protestant teachings in chapel and required to read the Protestant version of the Bible. He asked for her help, and she arranged for him to transfer to the Portsmouth Priory, a Catholic private school run by the Benedictine Order in Rhode Island. At Portsmouth Priory, the young Kennedy attended Mass more than the required three times a week, as well as compulsory morning and evening prayer services. He also served at times as an altar boy. All of this led his father to complain that "The boy is spending far too much time on religious subjects and not enough on academics."

As a young Catholic attending a Catholic school, Kennedy would have been steeped in the teachings of *The Baltimore Catechism*, which every Catholic school child of that era remembers memorizing. In the section on the Second Commandment mandate to love your neighbor as yourself, the catechism referred the student to the seven corporal works of mercy. Those, in turn, included "feed the hungry," "give drink to the thirsty," "clothe the naked," "shelter the homeless," and "visit the sick." The Catholic student was advised that "Every one is obliged to perform the works of mercy, according to his own ability and the need of his neighbor."

All of these focus on the poor and disadvantaged, and Kennedy's early religious education thus reinforced what he learned at home. He had a long-standing belief that he led a privileged life, and therefore owed a corresponding debt to those in need. He was reminded constantly by his parents as a child that there were others not as fortunate as he was, and he also taught his own children to help the less fortunate. In Indiana, after the assassination of Martin Luther King, he told some black leaders who visited him that "God's been good to me.... I just feel that if He's been that good, I should try to put something back in."

Kennedy remained serious about practicing his Catholic religion as an adult. He attended Mass every Sunday, prayed often, said the rosary, and went to confession. At times, he would also volunteer to be an altar boy if one failed to show up to serve Mass when he happened to be in attendance. He also liked to visit churches, and would tell his driver to stop at a Catholic church, where he would visit to say a prayer, or to go to confession. As a father of a large family, which ultimately included eleven children, one of whom was born after his death, he read to those at home every night from the Bible.

While Robert Kennedy practiced his religion, he frequently criticized the Catholic Church for being too parochial or conservative. At an early age, he refused to accept Father Leonard Feeney's preaching that there was no salvation outside the Catholic Church. As an adult, he lectured Pope Paul VI on the need for the Catholic Church to fight poverty and to assist Latinos and blacks in the United States and Africa. Kennedy also supported liberalized abortion laws.

Kennedy's strong sense of right and wrong approached

Manichaean proportions, and he did not retreat or equivocate in the face of opposition or apathy. When, for example, he was informed that a group of college students might not be interested in hearing him speak about hunger, he sharply replied that "If they don't care, the hell with them."

After the assassination of John Kennedy, Robert Kennedy's faith was challenged, and he struggled with how a good God could permit evil to prevail. Guided by Jacqueline Kennedy, he began to read and absorb the views of the Greek tragedians, coming to appreciate their understanding of suffering. He also began to read the works of Albert Camus, identifying with Camus's emphasis on the need for individual action and personal courage to confront the absurd. Kennedy's notebook is filled with quotations from Greek tragedies and Camus' work, and he often invoked both in his 1968 presidential campaign speeches. He did this most famously when he quoted Aeschylus to African-Americans in Indianapolis on the night of Martin Luther King's assassination.

Robert Kennedy's embrace of the Greek tragedians and Albert Camus did not cause the loss of his Catholic faith, but turned it instead toward a more Cross-centered spirituality. Indeed, his subsequent views on suffering and despair closely resemble those of the Spanish Catholic mystics, including St. John of the Cross, who said that "the endurance of darkness is preparation for great light," and that "God's greatest gifts fall into hearts that are empty of self."

Robert Kennedy's Policies

In reviewing the impact of his religion upon his public policies, we focus on the nearly five year period between the assassination of President John F. Kennedy and Robert Kennedy's own assassination, with particular emphasis upon Robert Kennedy's eighty two day presidential primary campaign in 1968. It was during this period that the mature Robert Kennedy emerged, with the conviction that he had to take action to alleviate the sufferings of others. His primary campaign proceeded on very familiar Catholic themes from the teachings on social justice. In his excellent study of Robert Kennedy's "politics of poverty," historian Edward Schmitt notes that Robert Kennedy followed the "Catholic ideals" of "concern for poverty, an emphasis on community and the common good, a preference for local initiative with the corresponding recognition that in the postwar world 'greater and higher' associations in the form of government may need to take action." In addition, Robert Kennedy saw many of the nation's problems as being rooted in a failure of respect for human dignity - a major aspect of Catholic social thought. In condemning violence while speaking to an African-American audience in Gary, Indiana, after the assassination of Martin Luther King, for example, Kennedy attributed the violence committed by young blacks to "a destructive and self-defeating attempt to assert [their] own worth and dignity as a human being."

Kennedy also saw a spiritual deficiency which afflicted the American people, referring to the need to remediate "the poverty of satisfaction - a lack of purpose and dignity - that inflicts us all." While campaigning in California, he characterized his campaign in these words: "Decency is at the heart of this whole campaign....Poverty is indecent. Illiteracy is indecent. The death, the maiming of brave young men in the swamps of Vietnam... that is also indecent. And it is indecent for a man to work with his back and his hands in the valleys of California without ever having hope of sending his son on to college. This is also indecent."

Here we will focus on four aspects of Robert Kennedy's public policies. They are ending the Vietnam War; eradicating poverty; eliminating racism; and empowering people to decide their own fate.

The Vietnam War

Kennedy's opposition to the Vietnam War was voiced in a distinctly moral, almost prophetic, voice. On the floor of the United States Senate on March 7, 1968, he questioned the hubris being exhibited by the United States, asking : "Are we like the God of the Old Testament that we can decide in Washington, D. C., what cities, what towns, what hamlets in Vietnam are going to be destroyed?" He continued questioning the war on moral grounds eleven days later in his first primary campaign speech, delivered at Kansas State University on March 18. There he asked, "Can we ordain to ourselves the awful majesty of God - to decide what cities and villages are to be destroyed, who will live and who will die, and who will join refugees wandering in a desert of our own creation?"

Kennedy also focused upon the loss of individual human lives, no matter what race or ethnic group an individual belonged to. In a lyrical speech in Sacramento in March of 1968, he said "While the sun shines in our sky, men are dying on the other side of the earth. Which of them could have come home and written a great symphony? Which of them could have come home to cure cancer? Which of them might have played in a World Series or given us the gift of laughter from the stage?"

His opposition to the Vietnam War was part of his campaign waged on behalf of the poor, minorities, and the underprivileged. This was because the war was being fought disproportionately by minorities, and also because the war diverted money needed by the poor. Kennedy chided white students at Idaho State, Indiana, and Creighton Universities, attacking the unfairness of student draft deferments, to rounds of student boos. At Indiana University, he lectured medical students, pointing out that "It's the poor who carry the major burden of the struggle in Vietnam. You sit here as white medical students, while black people carry the burden of the fighting in Vietnam." He also told Indiana University students in April of 1968 that "We cannot continue to deny and postpone the demands of our own people while spending billions in the name of the freedom of others."

POVERTY

Kennedy placed particular emphasis on the problems caused by poverty in America throughout his public career as a United States senator. In the course of Senate hearings on the problems of poverty held in 1967, Kennedy participated in several field trips, including one into the Mississippi Delta where he saw poverty that he considered worse than that he saw in 1960 in his brother's presidential primary campaign in that state. He also made many personal visits to migrant workers in California and to African-Americans living in poverty in many places across the United States. Cesar Chavez, the leader of the migrant workers in California and a staunch Kennedy ally, said that Robert Kennedy "could see things through the eyes of the poor."

In attacking poverty in a speech to students at the University of Kansas in March of 1968, Kennedy echoed Michael Harrington, noting that "If we believe that we, as Americans, are bound together by common concern for each other, then an urgent national priority is upon us. We must begin to end the disgrace of this other America." Kennedy pointed out that existing welfare programs were not the solution to poverty, again relying on the concern for protecting human dignity. He told the Americans for Democratic Action in January of 1966 that he saw welfare as having "destroyed self-respect and encouraged family disintegration." He favored in its place active participation by the poor in their own recovery. Again, this manifests a Catholic concern for the dignity of each individual rather than collective "solutions" that ignore the individual's worth and dignity. Throughout his 1968 campaign, Kennedy continued his attacks on the welfare system for its tendency to create dependency and be demeaning. He warned that "America could not survive... while millions of our people are slaves to dependency and poverty, waiting on the favor of their fellow citizens to write them checks."

Like Michael Harrington, who worked on Kennedy's campaign, Kennedy saw employment as the critical factor. He therefore worked with private business to promote jobs for the poor, proposing tax credits for new businesses begun in poor areas and tax deductions for part of the salaries paid to the very poor. Kennedy went further and called for the government to become the employer of last resort if private enterprise was unable to provide the number of jobs required. In a speech at the University of Alabama in March of 1968, he told students that "all...Americans must be freed by strong, determined national effort - not an effort which merely swells our budget with programs which will not free [the less fortunate of] Americans - but an effort which will provide jobs, not welfare dollars; decent homes, not slums standing on the foundation of federal indifference...."

Kennedy also promoted minimum wage and collective bargaining legislation to protect migrant workers, as part of his overall campaign to alleviate poverty in the United States.

RACISM

Kennedy opposed racism across the board, speaking against discrimination aimed at African-Americans, Latinos, and Native Americans. He had a near obsession with discrimination directed at Native Americans and scheduled ten of the seventy events held during the first months of his 1968 campaign at Native American venues despite the opposition of his campaign staff based on the low number of voters among Native Americans. In March of 1968, he spoke in Kansas of "Indians living on their bare and meager reservations, with no jobs, with an unemployment rate of 80 percent, and with so little hope for the future that for young men and women in their teens, the greatest cause of death is suicide." He even went on to compare Wounded Knee, the site of the 1890 massacre of Native Americans, to Dachau.

His concern for achieving human dignity for African-Americans was also a major thrust of Kennedy's policies. In his first speech after the assassination of John Kennedy, which he gave to The Friendly Sons of St. Patrick in Scranton, Pennsylvania, Robert Kennedy laced his presentation with Irish poems and stories, but went on to compare discrimination against blacks to that aimed at the Irish historically in both Ireland and America. He pointed out that "There are Americans who - as the Irish did - still face discrimination in employment - sometimes open, sometimes hidden. There are cities in America today that are torn with strife over whether a Negro should be allowed to drive a garbage truck; and there are walls of silent conspiracy to block the progress of others because of race or creed, without regard to ability." Even when he was urged to stress law and order in his Indiana campaign after the assassination of Martin Luther King, Kennedy combined a condemnation of violence with the message that white America needed to provide decent jobs for blacks to make them feel part of the country.

Robert Kennedy also championed the rights of Latinos, one of the very few white politicians to do so at the time. He told migrant farm workers at a March 1968 Mass of Thanksgiving marking the end of a twenty five day fast by their leader Cesar Chavez that "we will fight together to achieve for you the aspirations of every American: decent housing, decent schooling, a chance for yourselves and your children. You stand for justice and I am proud to stand with you."

EMPOWERMENT

Because of his concern for the common good of the entire American community, and the need to assure basic human dignity for all members of that broad community, Robert Kennedy championed a different type of federalism. He rejected the New Deal top-down model of federal control in favor of federal stimulation of, and assistance to, initiatives developed at the local level by a combination of local government, local authorities, and voluntary organizations.

In a Nebraska campaign speech delivered in April of 1968, Kennedy stated that "town-hall America may be gone; but there is no reason why small groups of people cannot plan for their own future, and decide their own fate, if government remembers how effective citizen participation can be. It is time - indeed, the time is long since passed - that the government begin to accommodate itself to the requirements of its citizens, instead of the other way around." He called for Washington to "return [the] power of decision to the American people in their own local communities."

Kennedy also called for regeneration of urban areas to be accompanied by education and full employment initiatives which were guided by inner city residents with the assistance of government, unions, universities, and the business community working together. He saw "the real answer" as being in "the full involvement of private enterprise system - in the creation of jobs, the building of housing, and provision of services, in training and education and health care."

As a United States senator from New York, Kennedy's major urban initiative had been the Bedford-Stuyvesant Project, aimed at alleviating poverty in a densely populated section of Brooklyn with a population of several hundred thousand which were mostly African-American but also included a large number of Puerto Ricans. Kennedy sponsored the formation of a development corporation with both a community board and a separate business board. He explained that "To turn promise into performance, plan into reality... we must combine the best of community action with the best of the private enterprise system. Neither by itself is enough; but in their combination lies our hope for the future."

Kennedy's focus upon the need for joint action at the local level by all interested parties is a refined and updated version of the Catholic social justice teaching regarding subsidiarity, which we discussed above in the Chapter on Al Smith. Robert Kennedy's approach echoed portions of Smith's message and appeal, but he went much further in a different America. Smith had principally appealed to urban immigrants, while Kennedy also reached out to include in a broad American tapestry African-Americans, Latinos, and Native Americans. Both Smith and Kennedy were skeptical about federal control and domination of programs designed to assist the poor. Smith looked instead to the primacy of state government to formulate programs to combat poverty. Kennedy, on the other hand, called for a new type of partnership of local citizens and other groups, including local government, voluntary organizations, and business groups to assist in community development and regeneration. While he recognized that the scope of the problems required federal funding and assistance, he insisted that those at the local level needed to formulate and implement the particularized programs appropriate to address the particular local problems they knew best.

CATHOLIC TRIBUNE OF THE PEOPLE

The evolution of Robert Kennedy from a "ruthless" political operative working on behalf of his older brother to a selfless tribune of the people finds much of its explanation in his self-examination after John Kennedy's assassination in November of 1963. Robert Kennedy was then only in his mid-thirties, and he was forced to move on. He did this first by winning a New York Senate seat in 1964, and thereafter by campaigning for the Democratic presidential nomination in 1968.

In that brief period of less than five years, Kennedy came to a deeper understanding of just how tragic life can be. He found his calling to be that of speaking on behalf of those who lacked a voice in the public square, and he drew on his Catholic faith in making this transformation. As Aeschylus said, in the quotation often repeated by Robert Kennedy, "In our sleep, pain which cannot forget falls drop by drop upon the heart until, in our own despair, comes wisdom through the awful grace of God."

Robert Kennedy's metamorphosis is well explained by the Spanish philosopher Miguel de Unamuno, who wrote in his *Tragic Sense of Life* that "many of the greatest heroes - perhaps the greatest of all, have been men of despair and... by despair they have accomplished their mighty works" because "out of this abyss of despair hope may arise, and... be the well-spring of human, profoundly human, action and effort, and of solidarity and even of progress."

PART IV

CATHOLIC JUDGES

AND AMERICAN LAW

CHAPTER NINE

CATHOLIC JUDGES AND HUMAN DIGNITY

"Social Justice can be obtained only in respecting the transcendent dignity of man. The person represents the ultimate end of society, which is ordered to him.... Respect for the human person entails respect for the rights that flow from his dignity as a creature.

Those rights are prior to society and must be recognized by it. They are the basis of the moral legitimacy of every authority: by flouting them, or refusing to recognize them in its positive legislation, a society undermines its own moral legitimacy."

The Catechism of the Catholic Church (1994)

"[O]ne must...choose *life*, and the things that favor life. This means respect for every living thing, but especially for every man, made in the image of God. Respect for man even in his blindness and in his confusion, even when he may do evil. For we must see that the meaning of man has been totally changed by the Crucifixion: every man is Christ on the Cross, whether he realizes it or not. But we, if we are Christians, must learn to realize it. That is what it means to be a Christian: not simply one who believes certain reports about Christ, but one who lives in a *conscious confrontation with Christ* in himself and in other men."

Thomas Merton

The influence of their religion upon the decisions of Catholic judges has become a controversial topic in the twenty first century, and some academics have suggested that Catholic judges are in fact more influenced in their decision-making by their religion than judges who follow other religions. Indeed, in a shockingly anti-Catholic cartoon in the *Philadelphia Inquirer* following the 2007 Supreme Court decision upholding a federal ban on partial-birth abortions which we discuss later in this Chapter, cartoonist Tony Auth portrayed the five justices – all Catholics – in the majority with bishops' mitres on their heads, mimicking the famous Thomas Nast cartoon of the nineteenth century showing bishops, with their mitres resembling alligator heads and jaws, swimming toward innocent school children whom they would indoctrinate with their growing system of parochial schools.

In this Chapter, we will review how judges from a Catholic background drew on concepts of the dignity of man to reach decisions protecting members of marginalized groups in American society. This is not to suggest that judges from different religious backgrounds (or with no religion at all) might not have come to the same decisions. What is important, however, is to examine how Catholic concepts affected these judges' reasoning in doing so.

WILLIAM GASTON AND THE RIGHTS OF SLAVES

In pre Civil War America, no person was more marginalized than the slave. Indeed, unlike the Northern abolitionist Protestants, the American Catholic Church was not then opposed to slavery as an institution. Remarkably, the Vatican did not officially condemn slavery as an institution until the Second Vatican Council in 1965. The Church's position on slavery before the Civil War was expressed by Francis Patrick Kenrick, who served as the Bishop of Philadelphia from 1830 to 1850. In an 1841 theology manual he wrote for use in his seminary, Kenrick quoted another theologian who had earlier explained that "slavery does not wipe out the equality of nature among human beings. In their view of slavery one person is conceived as the master of another such that the master holds a perpetual and total right to all the works of his servant. Even if it is right for one person to perform [labor] for another, by this particular law by which a master ought to take care of his servant, he must provide carefully to him all the obligations due to him by his nature....Slavery thus understood is not at odds with natural law in such a way that it might be considered a sin against natural law if a person holding slaves uses them moderately. Nevertheless, for the greatest good of the human race, slavery is endured with Christian kindness up to the present day among civilized nations."

Catholic laymen, including judges, and even some Catholic clergy owned slaves before the Civil War. Chief Justice Roger Taney of Maryland, the first Catholic to sit on the Supreme Court, inherited slaves, but freed them. He is notorious for writing the lead opinion in *Dred Scott v. Sanford* (1857), which held that blacks were not citizens of the United States, and that slaves were property of their master, with the master's property rights protected by the Fifth Amendment to the Constitution. The conclusion that slaves were but property of the master accorded with the laws of most southern states at the time, which generally viewed the slave as owing complete obedience to the master, and set no limits upon how the slave could be treated by the master or his delegate, subject only to the stricture that the life of the slave could not be taken.

One challenge to this view came from Justice William Gaston of the North Carolina Supreme Court. Gaston was one of the very few Catholics in that state. Indeed, Bishop John England of Charlestown, South Carolina, estimated in 1829 that there were only twenty-five Catholics in North Carolina, and no priests. Catholics were such a small minority that the North Carolina Constitution at that time limited office holding to adherents of "the truths of the Protestant religion." This stricture lasted until the North Carolina Convention of 1835, where Gaston tried to have the ban lifted, but succeeded only in having the word "Protestant" replaced by "Christian."

Gaston was a graduate of Princeton University, taking his degree first in his class. His father, a British Navy surgeon, had been active in the American Revolution and was shot dead in front of his wife and children in 1781 by British troops. Gaston – only three years old at the time of his father's death — was raised by his Irish Catholic mother, and was an active Catholic throughout his entire life. While he also owned slaves, he permitted one to run a blacksmith shop, and freed at least one other. At the 1835 Convention, he also spoke in favor of the right of suffrage for freed blacks, arguing that they should not be "politically excommunicated and have an additional mark of degradation fixed upon [them] solely on account of his color."

Gaston had a successful law practice and a wide-ranging political career. Before he was elected by the state legislature to a seat on the Supreme Court of North Carolina, he had served as a Federalist in both houses of the state legislature, as well as two terms in the United States House of Representatives.

Gaston is most remembered for his judicial opinion in *State v. Will* (1834), in which the conviction of a slave for the murder of an overseer and a death sentence imposed for that crime were reversed. The slave, Will, had run from the overseer and was shot in the back by him. Having survived the initial blast from a shotgun, he was pursued by the overseer and a struggle followed in which Will stabbed the overseer to death. While recognizing the doctrine that a slave was obliged to grant "[u]nconditional submission" to the master, Gaston nevertheless recognized an exception wherein "the slave has a right to defend himself against the unlawful attempt of his master to deprive him of life." He explained, in language reminiscent of Shakespeare in *The Merchant of Venice*, that:

> "If the passions of the slave be excited into unlawful violence by the inhumanity of a master...is it a conclusion of law that such passions must spring from diabolical madness? Unless I see my way clear as a sun beam, I cannot see that this is the law of a civilized people and of a Christian land. I will not presume an arbitrary and inflexible rule so sanguinary in its character, and so repugnant to the spirit of those holy statutes which 'rejoice the heart, enlighten the eye, and are true and righteous altogether.' *The prisoner is a human being, degraded indeed by slavery, but yet having organs, dimensions, senses, affections, and passions like our own.*" (Emphasis added)

One other significant opinion written by Gaston on the North Carolina Supreme Court was *State v. Manuel* (1838), in which he concluded that freed blacks were citizens of North Carolina. His opinion was later cited in the dissent of Justice Benjamin Curtis in the *Dred Scott* case.

William Gaston's arguments in favor of black suffrage, and for a slave's right to self defense, both were rooted in his strong Catholic beliefs, as manifested in his writings. Indeed, Thomas Morris, in his authoritative history of southern slavery and the law, expressly attributes the decision in *State v. Will* to Gaston's "deeply religious" views.

PIERCE BUTLER AND THE RIGHTS OF THE ACCUSED AND IMPAIRED

Legal historians have chosen to remember certain Justices who have served on the Supreme Court of the United States, and enshrine their names in America's history books. Pierce Butler has not been one of them. While most Americans have heard of John Marshall and Earl Warren, Butler is an unfamiliar name, even though he served on the Supreme Court for seventeen years and wrote over three hundred opinions. This disfavor stems from his assigned membership to the so-called "Four Horsemen," justices who opposed government regulation of business, and honored business' "freedom of contract" by striking down laws attempting to regulate workers' wages or hours. While this judicial philosophy reigned supreme in the late nineteenth and early twentieth centuries, it swiftly fell out of favor by the time of the New Deal. By continuing to apply these anti-regulation views to invalidate most of President Franklin D. Roosevelt's legislative victories in the First New Deal up to 1937, these justices and some others were attacked as reactionary, most harshly in a 1936 book coauthored by the muckraking journalist Drew Pearson and entitled *"The Nine Old Men."*

Butler deserves a better fate. As we will see, he stood firmly on the side of protecting the rights of the criminally accused long before the now familiar warning from *Miranda v. Arizona* (1966) became mandated. He also cast the sole vote against upholding the constitutionality of a Virginia statute permitting the sterilization of mentally handicapped individuals, a vote that was vindicated fifteen years later when a unanimous Supreme Court struck down a similar Oklahoma law in *Skinner v. Oklahoma* (1942).

Born on Saint Patrick's Day in 1866 to Irish Catholic immigrant parents, Pierce Butler spent his life before the Supreme Court in Minnesota. He served as county attorney for Ramsey County in that state from 1892 to 1897, prosecuting crimes. He then went into the private practice of law with several law firms in Minnesota, representing railroads and utilities as his major clients. James J. Hill, the railroad magnate and robber baron to reformers, was reputedly a friend, as well as a client. Butler was renowned as a fierce cross-examiner and was a dominating presence in the courtroom. This led to his selection by then President William Howard Taft's Attorney General in 1910 to represent the United States in antitrust lawsuits filed against flour millers, and in food and drug law prosecutions of meat packers. He was elected to head the Minnesota State Bar Association in 1908.

Although Butler was a life-long Democrat, he was nominated to the Supreme Court in 1922 by Republican President Warren G. Harding, on the suggestion of two Republicans - - Taft, who became Chief Justice in the preceding year, and Willis Van Devanter, who would join Butler in the "Four Horsemen." Butler's Catholic religion was attractive to Harding, since the late Chief Justice Edward White had been a Catholic and was replaced by the Protestant Taft. The sole other Catholic member of the Supreme Court at the time of Butler's appointment was Joseph McKenna, who had served on the court since 1898, and was suffering from mental decline in his last years on the court. McKenna would be pressured to resign, and did so in 1925. Justice Butler's Catholicism was so associated with his appointment that he was allegedly called the "Papal Delegate to the Supreme Court" by the Senate Press Gallery.

Butler's nomination met with opposition from both the left and the right. Liberals disliked him for his links to big business and his conservative philosophy, as well as for his role in expelling liberal members of the faculty of the University of Minnesota, on whose board of regents Butler sat. On the opposite side of the political spectrum, the Ku Klux Klan opposed the Butler nomination precisely because of his religion. As we have seen, the Second Klan had arisen in the early twentieth century in opposition to both Catholics and Jews, and the Klan produced 500,000 marchers on Washington, D.C. in 1925 to protest the potential selection by the Democratic Party of Al Smith, the Catholic New York Governor, to be its presidential nominee. Despite this opposition, Butler was confirmed by a vote of 61 to 8, with a remarkable 27 abstentions, presumably traceable to fear of angering the vigorous opposition elements. Butler became the fourth Catholic to serve on the Supreme Court, following two Chief Justices (Taney and White) and Justice McKenna.

We have already noted Butler's conservatism on the Supreme Court in areas of economic regulation, voting to strike down wage and hour laws and other governmental restrictions on business' "freedom of contract." Beyond these well-known cases, much of Butler's work on the court consisted of writing workmanlike, conservative opinions in the areas of public utility rate setting and tax law. Unlike his colleague Oliver Wendell Holmes, Butler eschewed the memorable phrase, choosing instead to review his draft opinions and excise anything he deemed too quotable.

While conservative on economic matters, Pierce Butler was remarkably liberal for his time in the area of the rights of the accused. He wrote that "Abhorrence, however great, of persistent and menacing crime, will not excuse transgression in the courts of the legal rights of the worst offenders." He implemented this view in a number of opinions expansively interpreting the protections of the Fourth Amendment against unreasonable searches and seizures, as well as the Sixth Amendment guarantee of the right to jury trial. His dissenting opinion in *Olmstead v. United States* (1928) is his most memorable in this area. There he voted with the Supreme Court liberals to find a Fourth Amendment violation where a conviction for conspiracy to violate the federal prohibition laws was largely based on telephone wiretaps which had been conducted without a warrant to do so. The majority opinion for five members of the court was written by Chief Justice Taft and joined by the other three of the "Four Horsemen." It held that telephone wiretaps did not fall within the Fourth Amendment protections because telephone wires were not part of a person's house, and therefore upheld the convictions.

In a separate dissent from those authored by the more liberal Justices, Butler called for a broad construction of the Fourth Amendment, believing that it "safeguards against all evils that are like and equivalent to those embraced within the ordinary meaning of its words." This construction, he argued, was "in harmony with the rule of construction that always has been applied to provisions of the Constitution *safeguarding personal rights....*" (Emphasis added.) Butler concluded that the defendants should be given a new trial.

As Chief Justice Charles Evans Hughes later put it, Butler was a "stickler for the rights of criminals." While it cannot be documented with certainty, Butler's sensitivity in this area is consistent with his staunch Catholic upbringing and beliefs. A lifelong practicing Catholic, he was a confidant of the Catholic hierarchy in Washington and was even asked to interview all the candidates for the position of Dean of the Catholic University Law School. The Church's concern for the rights and dignity of all individuals was certainly well known to Butler.

Outside the province of criminal law, Butler's Catholic faith is often cited as the explanation for his otherwise cryptic dissenting vote, without opinion, in *Buck v. Bell* (1927). There, speaking for a court which was unanimous except for Butler, Justice Holmes upheld the constitutionality of a Virginia statute which permitted the forced sterilization of the mentally deficient. Proclaiming that "Three generations of imbeciles are enough," Holmes opined that "It is better for all the world, if instead of waiting to execute degenerate offspring for crime, or to let them starve for their imbecility, society can prevent *those who are manifestly unfit* from continuing their kind." (Emphasis added) As we saw in the Prologue, this type of thinking flew straight in the face of Catholic doctrine, which opposed the "science" of eugenics, which was then quite fashionable among the elite in America, including Holmes.

It is unfortunate that Butler did not write an opinion to explain his dissenting vote, although we must remember that dissenting opinions were much rarer in those days than they are now, particularly where only one justice disagreed with the Opinion of the Court. Holmes, however, had no doubt about the source of Butler's opposition. According to Drew Pearson's 1936 book, *The Nine Old Men*, Butler was the last to vote on the case. While awaiting his reply to the draft opinion, Holmes allegedly said to an unnamed Justice that "I'll bet you Butler is struggling with his conscience as a lawyer on this decision. He knows the law is the way I have written it. But he is afraid of the Church. I'll lay you a bet the Church beats the law." Ultimately, however, as we noted above, it was Butler, not Holmes, who had "the law" right in 1927.

FRANK MURPHY AND THE INTERNMENT OF JAPANESE AMERICANS

When Pierce Butler died in November, 1939, he was replaced the following January by another Midwestern Irish Catholic, Frank

Murphy of Michigan. Murphy was named to what became known as "the Catholic seat" on the court by Franklin D. Roosevelt, and Murphy served for nine years until his death in 1949, when he was only fifty nine years old.

Murphy had a varied political career as a Democrat before he joined the Supreme Court. He had been a trial judge in Michigan, where he handled some famous cases, including two murder trials of African-Americans for the death of a white man who was part of a mob attack on an African-American doctor's home in a white neighborhood. Murphy was commended by the NAACP for his fairness, and went on to serve two terms as Mayor of Detroit, and as one as Governor of Michigan. As Governor, he refused to send in the National Guard to break up sit-in strikes by auto workers at the General Motors plant, and instead mediated that and other labor strikes in 1937. Between 1933 and 1936, he had held positions as Governor General and then High Commissioner to the Philippines, where he supported independence and women's suffrage in the islands. Murphy was an early Roosevelt supporter, and after Murphy was defeated for reelection as Michigan Governor, he was named Attorney General by Roosevelt in 1939. As Attorney General, Murphy instituted the first Civil Liberties Unit in the Department of Justice, and called for the creation of a system of federal public defenders. He was elevated to the high court within a year.

Murphy was an unabashed liberal, and probably was the most liberal Justice ever to serve on the Supreme Court of the United States. A member of both the ACLU and the NAACP, Murphy stated that his viewpoint was "reason and Christianity and Americanism." His Catholic faith was a large part of his life, so much so that a prominent Harvard official sneered that when Murphy joined the Supreme Court, he would bring with him as his colleagues the "Father, Son and Holy Ghost."

Murphy saw the Supreme Court as "the Great Pulpit," and announced that "[t]he old conception of the law as a system of purely negative rules designed primarily for the maintenance of order is giving way steadily to the broader view that the law is properly a *positive instrument for human betterment*." (Emphasis added). As a Supreme Court Justice, Murphy championed the rights of aliens, radical labor leaders, Jehovah's Witnesses, African Americans,

Japanese Americans, Native Americans, conscientious objectors, and criminal defendants. One Justice reportedly listed "F.M.'s Clients" as "Reds, Crooks, Indians and all other Colored People, Pacifists, Longshoremen, Japs, Women, Children, and Most Men." His affinity with these groups was so pronounced that Justice Felix Frankfurter reportedly described Murphy's loose construction of the law philosophy as "tempering justice with Murphy."

Murphy was particularly bold in his defense of the rights of Japanese American citizens and aliens during World War II, when both groups were relocated in the name of national security from the West Coast to internment camps. Murphy protested their treatment in his opinions in the so-called *Japanese Internment Cases*.

After the surprise Japanese attack on Pearl Harbor, Hawaii, on December 7, 1941, there were widespread fears of further attacks, this time directed at the West Coast of the continental United States. Based on these fears, military authorities requested the power to remove all Japanese Americans from the coastal areas. At the time, approximately 120,000 people of Japanese ancestry lived on the West Coast, and as many as seventy five percent may have been American citizens, not resident aliens. In California, one of every ten residents was Japanese American.

By February 1942, the military was authorized by executive order to exclude any person from designated military areas and those of Japanese, German, or Italian ancestry were ordered initially to stay out of large areas of the West Coast between 8 p. m. to 6 a. m. When many Japanese Americans moved from the coastal areas to avoid this curfew, freeze orders were issued in March 1942, requiring them first to remain in the area, and next to report to assembly centers. When they reported to these centers, they were sent to ten relocation centers as far away as Arkansas, without individual hearings or any opportunity to prove their loyalty to the United States. German and Italian Americans who were citizens of the United States were not subjected to such relocation en masse, but were permitted hearings to prove their loyalty where it was questioned.

While the Supreme Court never ruled on the legality of the relocation orders, it did review the constitutionality of both the curfew orders and the orders to report to assembly centers. In *Hirabayashi v. United States* (1943), a unanimous Supreme Court reviewed the criminal conviction of a University of Washington student of Japanese ancestry who had violated the curfew. Gordon Hirabayashi had never been to Japan and was an American citizen.

In an opinion by Chief Justice Harlan Stone, the conviction was upheld as a valid exercise of the power to wage war. Justice Murphy had prepared a dissenting opinion, but was persuaded by fellow Justices to join in the judgment. He then delivered a nominally concurring opinion which loudly protested the treatment of Japanese Americans. Murphy wrote that "[d]istinctions based on color and ancestry are utterly inconsistent with our traditions and ideals." He further observed that "[t]oday is the first time...that we have sustained a substantial restriction of the personal liberty of citizens of the United States based on the accident of race or ancestry. Under the curfew order here challenged no less than 70,000 Americans have been placed under a special ban and deprived of their liberty because of their particular racial inheritance. In this sense *it bears a melancholy resemblance to the treatment accorded to members of the Jewish race in Germany and in other parts of Europe.*" (Emphasis added). Murphy concluded by stating that he concurred in upholding the legality of the curfew only because of a strong military necessity which required immediate action because of the danger of imminent attack by the Japanese enemy, but warned that the curfew order "goes to the very brink of constitutional power."

The Supreme Court thereafter reviewed the constitutionality of the requirement that Japanese Americans leave the coastal areas and report to assembly centers in *Korematsu v. United States* (1944). While a majority of the court upheld this requirement, three Justices, including Murphy, dissented.

Murphy began his dissenting opinion by stating that exclusion of Japanese Americans from the Pacific Coast was unconstitutional and "falls into the ugly abyss of racism." Finding that the exclusion orders were based on "the erroneous assumption of racial guilt," he wrote that "[b]eing an obvious racial discrimination, the order deprives all those within its scope of the equal protection of the laws as guaranteed by the Fifth Amendment. It further deprives these individuals of their constitutional right to live and work where they will, to establish a home where they choose and to move about freely. In *excommunicating* them without benefit of hearings, this order also deprives them of all their constitutional rights to procedural due process. Yet no reasonable relation to an 'immediate, imminent, and impending' public danger is evident to support this racial restriction which is one of the most sweeping and complete deprivations of constitutional rights in the history of this nation in the absence of martial law." (Emphasis added).

Murphy's use of the word "excommunicating" is telling of his Catholic heritage. Indeed, as we saw earlier in this chapter, it is the same concept William Gaston employed when arguing for the rights of free blacks to vote in the 1835 North Carolina Convention. To excommunicate someone is to cut them off from the sacramental life of the Catholic Church, the equivalent of shunning in some Protestant denominations, and the religious equivalent of being sent off to, and isolated in, a leper colony. Use of this image illustrates how deeply Frank Murphy cared for the rights of those the powerful would marginalize and isolate from the chosen.

WILLIAM BRENNAN AND THE DEATH PENALTY

When Frank Murphy died in July of 1949, President Truman ignored the tradition of a "Catholic seat" on the Supreme Court, and appointed Tom Clark, a Texas Protestant who had been his Attorney General, to fill the vacancy. It would take seven years and four more appointments by Presidents Truman and Eisenhower before the next Catholic served on the court. Indeed, it was only after repeated requests to Eisenhower by Cardinal Francis Spellman of New York that a reliable Catholic be appointed that Eisenhower reached out to William Brennan, an Irish Catholic from New Jersey. Brennan was appointed to the court in 1956, and served there for thirty three years until his retirement in July of 1990. He died in 1997. Eisenhower reputedly said that the appointments of Brennan and Chief Justice Earl Warren were his two biggest mistakes as President.

William J. Brennan, Jr. was named after his father, an Irish immigrant who became a reformer and union official and went on to serve as Newark's Commissioner of Police and as a member of Newark's City Commission. The junior Brennan received superior educations at the University of Pennsylvania's Wharton School and at Harvard Law School. He joined the prominent Newark law firm of Pitney, Hardin & Ward, becoming the first Catholic lawyer hired by that firm. Because of his expertise in the newly important area of labor relations law, Brennan's name was later added to the name of the firm, being placed after that of Ward.

In 1949, Brennan became a trial judge in New Jersey, and was elevated in turn to the New Jersey appeals court and then to the state Supreme Court. He became a spirited critic of the anti-Communist activities of Senator Joseph McCarthy of Wisconsin, which came back to haunt him when McCarthy cast the only vote opposing Brennan's nomination to the Supreme Court of the United States.

At his confirmation hearing, Brennan was asked to respond to a question posed by the head of the National Liberal League regarding the potential influence of Brennan's Catholic faith on his decisions as a judge. He was asked whether as a judge he would "be able to follow the requirements of your oath or would you be bound by your religious obligations?" Answering a question that would be asked also of presidential candidate John F. Kennedy a few years later, Brennan replied that his oath to support the Constitution and laws of the United States would "alone" govern his actions on the Supreme Court. Brennan would carry out this commitment, even to the point of becoming a thorn in the side of the Catholic Church by his support for a constitutional right of a woman to have an abortion.

As an associate justice of the Supreme Court, Brennan followed in the liberal footsteps of Frank Murphy. He became a behind the scenes conciliator who formed coalitions to reach desired liberal results, often helping to draft opinions for other Justices, while changing his to accommodate differing views where possible. This outreach work included assisting Harry Blackmun in drafting his opinion in the controversial abortion rights case of *Roe v. Wade* (1973). It was Brennan who convinced Blackmun to embrace a privacy basis for the decision, and Brennan came up with the trimester approach laid down in the final opinion.

On the Supreme Court, Brennan was a consistent advocate of equal rights for women. One of his most significant opinions was *Craig v. Boren* (1976), which required sex-based classifications to be reviewed under a stricter constitutional scrutiny than previously had been the case. He also supported the Equal Rights Amendment. In the area of church and state, he voted for strict separation of the two spheres, including a ban on both compulsory prayer and Bible reading in public schools.

Brennan described his view of the Constitution as that of a charter which sets forth "a sparkling vision of *the supremacy of the human dignity of every individual,*" a value which he characterized as "transcendent." (Emphasis added). It is noteworthy that the quotation from the *Catholic Catechism* which heads this chapter would also refer to "the transcendent dignity of man," a phrase which incorporated a consistent teaching of the Church from many years before, and one which Brennan adopted wholeheartedly.

This focus on human dignity as the heart of the Constitution was most evident in Brennan's crusade against the death penalty, which he came over time to conclude was violative of the Eighth Amendment's ban on "cruel and unusual punishments." In his famous concurring opinion in *Furman v. Georgia* (1972), Brennan argued that the cruel and unusual punishments clause "prohibits the infliction of uncivilized and inhuman punishments. The State, even as it punishes, must treat its members with respect for their *intrinsic worth as human beings.* A punishment is 'cruel and unusual,' therefore, if it does not comport with *human dignity.*" (Emphasis added). He went on to contend that pain alone is not the standard because "the extreme severity of a punishment makes it *degrading to the dignity of human beings.*" (Emphasis added). Punishments such as the rack and other torture have been banned not only because of the extreme pain they inflict, but also because "they treat members of the human race as nonhumans, as objects to be toyed with and discarded. They are thus inconsistent with the fundamental premise of the [cruel and unusual punishments] Clause that *even the vilest criminal remains a human being possessed of common human dignity.*" (Emphasis added). Brennan dissented in every case upholding a death penalty sentence thereafter, recording his constitutional opposition to the death penalty in almost 2000 cases.

Brennan's words and approach closely parallel those of Pope John Paul II in St. Louis, Missouri, more than twenty five years later, on January 27, 1999. In his homily at a papal Mass celebrated in that city, he stated that:

"The new evangelization calls for followers of Christ who are unconditionally pro-life: who will proclaim, celebrate and serve the

Gospel of life in every situation. A sign of hope is the increasing recognition that *the dignity of human life must never be taken away, even in the case of someone who has done great evil.* Modern society has the means of protecting itself, without definitively denying criminals the chance to reform.... I renew the appeal I made most recently at Christmas for a *consensus to end the death penalty, which is both cruel and unnecessary.*" (Emphasis added).

As a justice of the Supreme Court, William Brennan followed his oath to apply the Constitution and laws of the United States as he understood them, sometimes at odds with the official teachings of his Catholic faith, as was the case with his votes in favor of abortion rights. In the case of the death penalty and his general view of the Constitution as "a sparkling vision of the supremacy of the human dignity of every individual," however, Brennan's legal philosophy aligned well with the most fundamental tenets of his faith.

ANTHONY KENNEDY: ABORTION, CRIMINAL PUNISHMENT, GAY RIGHTS, AND HUMAN DIGNITY

Catholic concepts of human dignity have most often been invoked in Supreme Court opinions by Justice Anthony Kennedy. Before his appointment to the Supreme Court, Kennedy was a California lawyer in private practice and a constitutional law teacher at the McGeorge School of Law at the University of the Pacific. A conservative Republican and a Catholic, Kennedy worked for Ronald Reagan when Reagan was Governor of California. At Reagan's suggestion, President Gerald Ford appointed Kennedy to the Ninth Circuit federal Court of Appeals in 1975. He was nominated to the Supreme Court late in 1987 by President Reagan after two earlier nominations had been defeated (Robert Bork) or withdrawn (Douglas Ginsburg).

Particularly after the resignation of Justice Sandra Day O'Connor in 2006, Kennedy became the swing vote on close cases in the Supreme Court. Vitually all of the current Supreme Court watchers consider Kennedy to be the critical justice to persuade in cases posing important issues of constitutional law; indeed, many briefs are written with targeted appeals to his views as expressed in his previous opinions. Given this status, there are some who consider him the most powerful person in the United States since Justice O'Connor's retirement.

Edward F. Mannino

Kennedy has sided with the liberal wing of the Supreme Court on such issues as the rights of enemy combatants and the banning of school prayer, while joining the conservative wing on the appropriate use of race in student public school assignment and some criminal law issues. Kennedy typically writes his own separate opinions, spelling out his particularized views of the issues, which facilitates and encourages lawyers to discuss his specific views in their briefs.

Justice Kennedy has appealed to concepts of human dignity to support his views in several areas of constitutional law. These include abortion, criminal punishment, and gay rights, each of which is discussed separately below.

Abortion: With the exception of the years from 1898 to 1921, when Edward White and Joseph McKenna served together, the norm was that there would be only one Catholic justice at a time on the Supreme Court. When William Brennan took his seat in 1956, he became only the sixth Catholic to serve on the court. The norm changed, however, late in the twentieth century, beginning with the appointment of Antonin Scalia by President Ronald Reagan in 1986. By the time Samuel Alito joined the court in 2006, there were five Catholic Justices - a majority of the court (by 2009, there were six). This led the British journal *The Economist* to refer to the Supreme Court as the "Papal Court," and decisions on abortion rights became the object of strict scrutiny by those who continued to fear the influence of Catholicism on its judicial adherents. When *Gonzales v. Carhart* (2007) cut back on abortion rights with the five-person majority consisting of the five Catholic Justices, the *Philadelphia Inquirer* went so far as to run a cartoon depicting the Supreme Court bench with the five Catholics wearing bishops' mitres, and some law professors, bloggers, and media personalities contended that the result was faith-driven. In reality, as most fair-minded commentators agreed, the abortion decisions reflected the conservative judicial philosophies of the justices rather than their religion. Catholic justices have been both liberal (Justices Murphy and Brennan) and conservative (Justices Scalia, Alito, Clarence Thomas, and Chief Justice John Roberts), and libertarian or a little bit of both. The latter is a good description for Anthony Kennedy.

On abortion, Kennedy has swung back and forth between the

liberals and conservatives by both upholding the general concept of a constitutional right for women in making reproductive decisions, and by also placing limitations upon exercise of that right. In *Planned Parenthood v. Casey* (1992), most notably, he was a moving force in the lead plurality opinion which declined to overrule *Roe v. Wade*, while at the same time embracing a more conservative "undue burden" standard for deciding the constitutionality of restrictions on abortion. But despite refusing to overrule *Roe*, Kennedy later voted in dissent with the conservative minority to uphold the Nebraska statutory ban on partial birth abortion in *Stenberg v. Carhart* (2000). Seven years later, he authored the majority opinion upholding a federal ban on partial birth abortion in *Gonzales v. Carhart* (2007), the case which generated the Catholic justices controversy mentioned above.

Stenberg and *Gonzales* dealt with a particularly barbaric method of abortion in which "the fetus is killed just inches before completion of the birth process" (*Gonzales*), and in which the fetus "bleeds to death as it is torn limb from limb" (*Stenberg*). Kennedy's opinions in the two cases focused on the absence of any sense of *"respect for life"* in the process, and concluded that government had an interest in banning it completely. He wrote in *Gonzales* that:

"The Act's ban on abortions that involve partial delivery of a living fetus furthers the Government's objectives. No one would dispute that, for many, [the partial birth abortion] process is a procedure itself laden with *the power to devalue human life*. Congress could... conclude that the type of abortion proscribed by the Act requires specific regulation because it implicates additional ethical and moral concerns that justify a special prohibition. Congress determined that the abortion methods it proscribed had a 'disturbing similarity to the killing of an unborn infant.'" (Emphasis added).

Earlier, in his dissenting opinion in *Carhart*, Kennedy had similarly concluded that "States also have an interest in forbidding medical procedures which, in the State's reasonable determination, might cause the medical profession or society as a whole to become *insensitive, even disdainful, to life, including life in the human fetus*. Abortion...has consequences beyond the woman and her fetus." (Emphasis added).

Kennedy's vote not to overrule *Roe v. Wade* is consistent with his votes to uphold bans on partial birth abortion, since both reflect conservative legal positions, rather than religious faith. The *Planned Parenthood* plurality opinion upholding *Roe* was based partially on a conservative respect for not tampering with settled precedent, while the partial birth abortion opinions reflected a conservative respect for the rights of state and federal governments to legislate restrictions on conduct based on "ethical and moral concerns" in areas of legitimate public interest. Nevertheless, Kennedy found support for his opinions on partial birth abortion in Catholic teachings regarding the dignity of every human person, born and unborn.

Criminal Punishment: Kennedy has relied most often on concepts of human dignity in the area of criminal punishment, placing constitutional limitations upon the imposition of various forms of punishment, including the death penalty and life imprisonment without the possibility of parole, as well as on conditions of confinement, all based on the impact of those punishments or conditions on the dignity of the prisoner.

Kennedy has not been an opponent of the death penalty on constitutional grounds, except in certain defined areas. He has voted to uphold the death penalty in numerous cases despite Catholic teaching against it. Indeed, it was the same five Catholic justice majority that he was part of in *Gonzales v. Carhart* that also voted to uphold the imposition of the death penalty in *Kansas v. Marsh* (2006), even where the aggravating and mitigating circumstances juries were required to balance before voting for death were equally balanced. Moreover, another Catholic justice, Antonin Scalia, wrote a blistering concurring opinion in that case in favor of upholding the death penalty, ridiculing "sanctimonious criticism" by foreign commentators, and contending that the American people had decided that the good gained from deterrence and the meting out of justice for horrible criminal action justified capital punishment.

Kennedy has, however, voted to strike down as unconstitutional any imposition of the death penalty where the defendants were juvenile offenders, mentally disabled, or child rapists (where death did not result from the rape). These decisions were predicated on the Eighth Amendment's prohibition against the imposition of "cruel and unusual punishments." In the nineteenth century decisions of the Supreme Court interpreting this provision, it was seen only as prohibiting certain barbaric *methods* of punishment such as the rack, which involved either torture or a lingering death. That interpretation was expanded in *Weems v. United States* (1910), in an opinion for four members of the court written by a Catholic Justice, Joseph McKenna, to include punishments which were deemed to be excessive or disproportionate to the offense committed. *Weems* dealt with an appeal from the Philippine Islands, where a Coast Guard official involved in a minor falsification of public documents was sentenced to fifteen years imprisonment "at hard and painful labor," was compelled to "always carry a chain at the ankle, hanging from the wrists," and was prohibited from receiving any "assistance whatsoever from without the institution." In addition, certain "accessory penalties" were imposed, including lifetime surveillance, deprivation of all parental rights, prohibition from holding any public office, and loss of voting rights. In declaring the punishments unconstitutionally cruel and unusual, McKenna characterized them as "tormenting," oppressive, and of a nature which deprived the prisoner of "essential liberty." He observed that "No circumstance of degradation is omitted."

By the time of Kennedy's opinions discussed here, the approach taken by McKenna in *Weems* had been expanded and utilized to strike down several other punishments as constitutionally excessive. In *Graham v. Florida* (2010), which struck down as unconstitutional the imposition on a juvenile of life imprisonment without the possibility of parole for a non-capital crime, Kennedy explained that this line of precedent embodied "a <u>moral judgment</u>," and reflected "the essential principle that, under the Eighth Amendment, the State must respect the <u>human attributes</u> even of those who have committed serious crimes." Kennedy used the same Eighth Amendment authority to write previous majority opinions declaring unconstitutional any imposition of the death penalty on individuals who were eighteen or under at the time of the crime (*Roper v. Simmons* (2005)), and imposition of the death penalty on child rapists of any age where death had not resulted (*Kennedy v. Louisiana* (2008)). In *Kennedy v. Louisiana*, Justice Kennedy explained that "Evolving standards of decency must embrace and express respect for the <u>dignity of the person</u>, and the punishment of criminals must conform to that rule." Moreover, imposition of the death penalty threatens the law's "sudden descent into brutality, transgressing the constitutional commitment to decency and restraint." Decency, in turn, "in its essence, presumes respect for the individual and thus moderation or restraint in the application of capital punishment."

Justice Kennedy has also found Eighth Amendment violations in the terms and conditions of imprisonment. In *Brown v. Plata* (2011), his majority opinion for the Supreme Court concluded that "A prison that deprives prisoners of basic sustenance, including adequate medical care, is incompatible with the concept of human dignity and has no place in civilized society." This is so because "Prisoners retain the essence of human dignity inherent in all persons." He also dissented from an interpretation of the federal sentencing statute in *Barber v. Thomas* (2010) that increased the time of imprisonment for almost 200,000 prisoners, noting that the manner in which he would interpret the sentencing statute implemented the statutory purpose of giving prisoners "incentive for good behavior and dignity from its promised reward."

Gay Rights: Just as Justice Brennan's liberal judicial philosophy aligned with the Catholic opposition to the death penalty as inconsistent with human dignity, Justice Kennedy's philosophy aligned with the Catholic Church's "respect for life" teachings on abortion and criminal punishment. But Kennedy has also employed the concept of human dignity in voting to protect conduct opposed to Catholic doctrine. Thus, Kennedy wrote the majority opinion striking down the criminalization of private, consensual homosexual conduct in *Lawrence v. Texas* (2003), despite Catholic doctrine opposing such conduct. In his opinion, Kennedy characterized the criminalization of private homosexual intercourse as placing a "stigma" on gay people, and saw criminalization as having significant import "for the *dignity* of the persons charged." In his view, upholding the criminalization of "intimate [gay] conduct" as constitutional, as the Supreme Court had done in a previous opinion that was overruled by *Lawrence*, "*demeans* the lives of homosexual people."

Viewed in an overall context, Kennedy's opinions reveal a use of the concepts of human dignity that is consistent with a conservative, but libertarian, jurisprudence. Although not always predictable, Kennedy's rulings have a logical consistency which draw on both a conservative judicial philosophy of restraint and deference to governmental action and a personal commitment to protecting human dignity which is informed by his Catholic beliefs.

CATHOLIC JUDGES AND HUMAN DIGNITY

What, if anything, do the references in their opinions to Catholic concepts of human dignity tell us about the Catholic judges we have reviewed in this chapter? To answer this question, we must recall that the specific concepts on which they drew varied from one judge to another, and were utilized by each judge to *explain* the reasoning of his decisions. I have argued elsewhere that Supreme Court justices are most affected in their decision making by the dominant political culture of their times. This analysis applies fully as well to those judges we have examined here. Thus, conservative judges Pierce Butler, Antonin Scalia, Clarence Thomas, Samuel Alito, and Chief Justice John Roberts were each appointed by a conservative Republican president (Harding, Reagan, and the two Bushes), and four of them served as lawyers or agency head in those or later Republican administrations. Liberal Justice Frank Murphy was President Franklin D. Roosevelt's Attorney General, while Justice William Brennan turned out as a surprise to President Eisenhower. Other than Justice Brennan, they each generally reflected in their decisions the conservative or liberal political culture of their respective times.

Catholic concepts of how human dignity should be protected embrace a variety of specific applications. What each application has in common, as Richard John Neuhaus has explained, is "protect[ing] those who lack autonomy, or whose autonomy is gravely limited." Conservative judges can draw upon natural law moral concepts of human dignity such as the prohibition of abortion in favor of the right to life of the unborn fetus, while liberal judges can accept more readily social justice concepts of human dignity, such as opposition to the death penalty. This divergence explains how Catholic judges can at times appear to be following Church teachings in their decision making, while also voting for results in other cases which contravene other teachings. Thus, judges will explain conservative or liberal outcomes by drawing upon those Catholic concepts of human dignity which resonate with their judicial philosophies and align with the results reached in their opinions. Using these concepts also may resonate with Catholic readers of such opinions. In some cases, such as with Justice Anthony Kennedy, Catholic concepts of human dignity will be extended so as to protect conduct condemned by Catholic teaching, again in service of a broader judicial philosophy which draws on both Catholic teachings and other influences. The "explaining" function of judicial opinions offers an opportunity for all judges to draw upon the whole of their background, including any religious beliefs, to advocate for the result they have reached. In the end, what is clear is that Catholic justices will at times draw selectively on the teachings of their religion to justify decisions that they announce, setting forth the principles underlying those teachings as worthy of respect by both judge and citizen.

PART V

RELIGIOUS SISTERS

IN AMERICAN SOCIETY

CHAPTER TEN

SISTERS OF COMPASSION: HOW AMERICAN NUNS

HELP THE HELPLESS

NUNS IN AMERICAN SOCIETY

Nuns have long been an underappreciated treasure in American Catholicism. While they are best known for having educated hundreds of thousands of Catholic schoolchildren, particularly in the mid-20th century, their ministry has been far broader, and started in the United States in the late 18th century. That ministry has extended to serving the poor, the sick, the aged, the disabled, and minorities in many ventures through a variety of orders, running hospitals, orphanages, homes, and providing a wide range of social services. In the American Civil War, for example, one of five nurses on both sides was a nun, and their ministries were vital to binding up the War's wounds, both physical and spiritual. One Maine Union soldier, himself a Protestant, confided to his journal that "I am far from being a Roman Catholic. But from what I have seen during this war, I am convinced that the Roman Catholics have done more for sick and wounded soldiers North and South than any other religious sect." Nuns were key movers in setting up education, health care, and social services for settlers in the American West in the 19th century. They were also active in educating and caring for Native Americans, again going back to the mid-19th century, particularly in the West.

American nuns are well-educated. They have done significant scholarly work in America, and have produced several noted theologians. As of 2010, nearly sixty percent of American nuns started in religious life with an undergraduate degree, while twenty-five percent possess a graduate degree. Nuns are also racially and ethnically diverse. While sixty percent are white, twenty percent are

Asian, ten percent are Latino, and six percent are African-American. The number of nuns has, however, fallen drastically in the last forty years. In 1968, there were approximately 180,000 nuns in the United States; by 2003, that number had shrunk almost two-thirds, to about 65,000, with a median age of 69. In 2011, only 56,000 nuns remained, and more than ninety percent were at least sixty years old. This decline in the number of nuns has, in turn, contributed to a sharp drop in the number of Catholic parochial schools, universities, and hospitals, particularly in areas serving the urban poor. The leadership of Catholic hospitals has also changed since the 1960s. While some 770 of 796 Catholic hospitals were led by nuns or priests in 1968, by 2011, only eight of the remaining 636 Catholic hospitals had a nun or priest at their head.

In this Chapter, we review the ministries of four American nuns who aided the poor, the sick, the mentally ill, the homeless, and minorities from the 18th to the 21st centuries. Remarkably, two of these women were married with children, becoming nuns after their husbands died.

ELIZABETH SETON

Elizabeth Ann Bayley Seton was the first American-born citizen who was named a saint. Canonized in 1975 by Pope Paul VI, she was an unlikely candidate for Catholic sainthood at the time of her birth in 1774. She was born in New York to an Episcopalian family, and her mother, who died when Elizabeth was only three years old, was the daughter of an Episcopal minister. Elizabeth was married at the age of nineteen to William Magee Seton, and they had five children.

Mother Seton, as she later was known, was a deeply religious Episcopalian, and was active in charitable ventures from early adulthood. She was one of the founders of the Society for the Relief of Poor Widows with Children, which began in New York in 1787. Her involvement with this charity is particularly ironic, since she became a poor widow with children herself fifteen years later.

William Seton was a businessman involved in the shipping industry. Unfortunately, his firm went bankrupt in 1800 and he became ill with tuberculosis. The Seton family traveled to Italy in an attempt to ameliorate William's illness, but he died in Italy in 1803, when Elizabeth was only twenty nine years old. During their stay in Italy, the Setons were befriended by the Filicchi family, and Elizabeth remained friends with them for the rest of her life, communicating with them by letter over many years. In large part because of their friendship, Elizabeth Seton converted to Catholicism in 1805, after her return to the United States. Her conversion followed a period of study of Catholicism, aided by the Fillichis. She wrote to them that "I will go peaceably and firmly to the Catholic Church: for if Faith is so important to our salvation, I will seek it where true Faith first began, seek it among those who received it from God Himself."

Seton's conversion was a scandal to her Episcopalian family, and the rampant anti-Catholic prejudice of the times, which we covered at length in the Prologue, led to her having great difficulty finding work to support her and her five children. Initially, she began a boarding house for New York schoolboys, but ultimately relocated to the state of Maryland, at the invitation of the Sulpician Order of Catholic priests. They assisted her and encouraged her to open a Catholic school for girls in Emmitsburg, Maryland, where the Sulpicians had a seminary. In 1808, Seton founded St. Joseph's Academy and Free School in Maryland. Originally intended for the education for poor girls, it began instead to educate the well-to-do, because of financial constraints incurred in starting the school. Seton's work in founding St. Joseph's is considered by many to be the foundation of the American Catholic school system, which did not begin in earnest until the mid-19th century.

In the following year, Seton founded a religious order of nuns, which were known as the Sisters of Charity of St. Joseph. The mission of the order was to help the children of the poor. To that end, the sisters visited the sick and poor and provided care for them as part of their ministry. Their work included taking over the operations of orphanages in Philadelphia in 1814, and in New York in 1817. The order also began a school in Philadelphia in 1818.

Mother Seton died in 1821 of tuberculosis - the same disease that had taken her husband. She was only forty six years old at the time, and she left behind three of her five children, whom she had continued to care for during her years as a nun. Her other two children had died prematurely. After Seton's death, her successors opened a number of hospitals, and devoted themselves to a wide range of social work. Seton Hall University in New Jersey is named after her. It was founded by her half nephew in 1856. He was then Bishop of Newark and later became the Archbishop of Baltimore.

ROSE HAWTHORNE

Born in 1851 in Lenox, Massachusetts, Rose Hawthorne was the daughter of the famous novelist Nathaniel Hawthorne. In her youth, she became acquainted with many of the members of the Transcendentalist Movement, including Ralph Waldo Emerson, Henry David Thoreau, and Herman Melville. Like Elizabeth Seton, she was born and raised a Protestant.

From 1853 to 1860, when the American Civil War broke out, Hawthorne lived in England and Italy with her family after her father was named U. S. Consul to England. She had little formal education, and both of her parents died when she was still a teenager. After her return to the United States, she married George Parsons Lathrop in an Anglican ceremony when she was only twenty years old. He was then an assistant editor at the Atlantic Monthly, and she followed in her father's footsteps by writing short stories and poems. Mrs. Lathrop had one child, Francis, who was born in 1876. Unfortunately, he died of diptheria at the age of five.

To the great dismay of their Transcendentalist friends, the Lathrops, like Mother Seton before them, converted to Catholicism in 1891. Because George Lathrop was an alcoholic, their marriage failed, and they separated in 1895 after nearly twenty five years of marriage. George Lathrop died in 1898, and Rose Hawthorne radically changed her life in the 1890s. She began to work with patients who had incurable cancer, inspired to do so after reading biographies of Saint Rose of Lima, who worked with the poor and sick in Peru, and of Father Damian, who moved in with, and cared for, lepers in their colony in Hawaii. Hawthorne took up this work after she read an account of a poor seamstress who had died of cancer after having been sent to Blackwell's Island in New York. It was the analogue of the Hawaiian leper colony of Father Damian, since at that time, cancer was considered to be a contagious disease like leprosy, and its victims were often quarantined.

Hawthorne took a three-month course in nursing from a cancer hospital and moved to the slums of New York, on the Lower East Side. There she went to the homes of poor cancer patients, and often took them into her own apartment to bathe, feed, and care for them. She wrote that "A fire was…lighted in my heart, where it still burns….I set my whole being to endeavor to bring consolation to the cancerous poor." In 1899, she founded St. Rose's Free Home for Incurable Cancer, named after Saint Rose of Lima, and she became a Dominican nun in 1900. In 1901, she opened the Rosary Hill Home in Hawthorne, New York.

Like Mother Seton, Rose Hawthorne began an order of nuns. In 1906, she became Mother Mary Alphonsa of the Dominican Sisters, Congregation of St. Rose of Lima. The nuns of the order, then as now, cared for the destitute with incurable cancer. They do not accept any money from the patients or their families for this care, nor do they accept government payments. Rose Hawthorne worked with terminally-ill cancer patients for thirty three years, starting six homes in the United States devoted to this mission. She called on well-to-do contacts she had made as the daughter of Nathaniel Hawthorne, and received financial assistance to support her ministry from some famous writers, including Mark Twain.

Rose Hawthorne died in 1926, at the age of seventy five. She has been named a Servant of God, the first step on the road to sainthood, and the Catholic Catechism for Adults starts its Chapter 6, which treats the subject of Human Dignity, with a note on her life and ministry. Nevertheless, she is the least well known of the four sisters who are the subjects of this Chapter, and does not even have a biographical entry in most Catholic publications dealing with the history of American Catholicism.

KATHERINE DREXEL

When Katherine Drexel was declared a saint in 2000, Pope John Paul II observed that "Katherine Drexel is an excellent example of that practical charity and generous solidarity with the less fortunate which has long been the distinguishing mark of American Catholics." The second American-born saint, Drexel was a rich heiress who devoted her life and her fortune to Native Americans and African-Americans.

Katherine Drexel was born into a prominent and wealthy family in 1858. Her father, Francis Drexel, was one of the three brothers who were partners in the prominent investment bank known as Drexel & Company, which was headquartered in Philadelphia. The Drexel firm was perhaps the most prominent in the United States at that time. Indeed, the Drexels formed a partnership with the young J.P. Morgan in 1871, where they were the more prominent and wealthier partners in what was known as Drexel, Morgan & Company.

Katherine Drexel's mother died shortly after her birth, and her father remarried a few years later. His second wife, Emma Bouvier, was an ancestor of Jacqueline Kennedy; one of Emma's brothers was Kennedy's great-grandfather. Emma Drexel was a great influence upon the three Drexel children. She was an extremely religious Catholic, as was her husband Francis. Mrs. Drexel was generous to the poor, and opened the Drexel Philadelphia home three times a week to give money, food, and clothing to the poor of Philadelphia. She gave what was then the enormous sum of $20,000 a year in these charitable distributions.

Katherine and her sisters were also given a strong religious education by their pious parents. Emma Drexel conducted Sunday evening seminars on the saints for the children, who were particularly fond of St. Francis of Assisi. The Drexel home had a home oratory, with an altar, crucifix and candles, and the Drexels said the rosary and evening prayers together each day.

After her father and stepmother, the second great influence on Katherine Drexel was Bishop James O'Connor. O'Connor had been the head of St. Charles Seminary in Philadelphia, but was exiled to the suburbs after a disagreement with Archbishop Wood of that city. In the suburbs, he was pastor of a church in the area in which the Drexels had a ninety acre farm. He became friendly with the Drexel family and started a mentoring relationship with Katherine when she was only fourteen years old. He continued to act as her spiritual adviser until his death. He was named Bishop of Omaha in 1876, with jurisdiction over the Dakotas and Wyoming, where many Native American tribes resided at that time.

Katherine and her sisters led a life of luxury, including travel both within the United States and to Europe. In September 1874, for example, the Drexels began a six-month trip to Europe, where they visited not only the usual tourist attractions, but also numerous cathedrals and the shrine at Lourdes. They also had a private audience with Pope Pius IX.

Emma Drexel died in 1883, after a long and painful illness caused by cancer. Katherine had been struggling with whether she should become a nun and wrote a letter to Bishop O'Connor in 1883, enclosing a chart which set out the pros and cons of her following a religious vocation. In her analysis, she expressly noted that she would be deprived of future luxuries and might be forced to submit to a "stupid" superior with a "thorough want of judgment." Katherine Drexel's correspondence reveals an extremely intelligent, well-educated, and articulate individual, who typically exhibited a refreshing candor.

Francis Drexel died in 1885, leaving Katherine and her sisters as extremely wealthy orphans. Katherine was then in her mid twenties, and she and her sisters were left ninety percent of her father's $14 million estate, an enormous fortune both then and now. Francis Drexel structured their interest in his estate so that each of the sisters received only an equal share of the income generated by the principal annually. Upon the death of any sister, the remaining sisters or sister would receive the share of the deceased, with the last surviving sister receiving all of the income. Katherine, who lived to be 97, ultimately received all of the income from the estate left by her father, and devoted it all to the work of her religious order. On her death, the principal was distributed to charities her father had named in his will, who had received the other ten percent of the estate in 1885.

Shortly after their father's death, the sisters were inundated with requests to fund multiple charities from their inheritances. They were visited, among many others, by Catholic Indian missionaries who requested that they fund the building of Indian schools, which the sisters agreed to do. The United States bishops had appealed for help for both Native American and African-American missions in the previous year, and those missions became an important part of the Catholic Church's outreach in America thereafter. Katherine and her sisters were familiar with Native American poverty from their family trips to the American West in their early years, and Katherine was especially interested in the welfare of American Indians from those early days.

When Katherine was on a trip to Italy in 1887, she had a private audience with Pope Leo XIII. She asked the Pope to supply missionaries for the schools she was then financing for Native Americans. In reply, Leo suggested that she herself become a missionary, a suggestion which made her cry at the time. Following her return to the United States, Katherine spent much of the next two years visiting Indian missions in the Midwestern United States. At that point, she decided to become a nun herself.

Katherine Drexel entered the novitiate of the Sisters of Mercy in 1889. She was then 30 years old. Thereafter, in 1891, she founded her own order, the Sisters of the Blessed Sacrament for Indians and Colored People, with the mother house located in Cornwell Heights, Pennsylvania, near the site of the Drexel family farm. By the end of 1891, the order had twenty eight novices.

In addition to her interest in Native Americans, Katherine Drexel and her sisters also assisted the Catholic Church's mission to African-Americans. In 1886 and 1887, Katherine Drexel had provided money to start a black parish and a black school in Philadelphia. Her work spread beyond that city when she was contacted by Archbishop Francis Janssens of New Orleans, who sought her financial support for his diocese's mission to African-Americans, which then included thirty two schools for black children, with an additional four schools in the planning stage. Drexel provided funds which aided the missions for blacks in New Orleans until Janssens' death in 1897. Thereafter, after the passage of several years, Drexel resumed her activities in Louisiana, and her order's mission grew there, eventually making it the largest apostolate of the Sisters of the Blessed Sacrament.

Katherine was not the only Drexel who assisted African-Americans financially. Her younger sister, whose married name was Louise Morrell, was a significant supporter of black causes. Louise founded a school for blacks outside of Richmond, Virginia in 1894, and also provided financial assistance to the Josephite Fathers, whose mission was and is to serve the African-American community. Louise named her Virginia school St. Emma's, in honor of her stepmother. Katherine began a second school on an adjoining property in 1895, naming it St. Francis de Sales, in honor of her father.

Katherine Drexel took a special fourth vow for her order, added to the usual vows of poverty, chastity and obedience taken by other

Catholic orders. That vow was "To be the mother and servant of the Indian and Negro races....and not to undertake any work which would lead to the neglect or abandonment of the Indian and Colored races." She also urged that the Catholic Church establish a special board to supervise its mission work for African-Americans. This was done in 1905.

Katherine Drexel financed the construction of convents and schools in twenty six dioceses across the country to serve both Native Americans and African-Americans, starting with St. Catherine's School for Native Americans in Santa Fe, New Mexico. Drexel paid for the land and buildings erected for the Indians, and then deeded them over to Catholic Indian Bureau, always doing so anonymously. Drexel's efforts to build schools for blacks met much opposition in South from both white citizens who opposed blacks being educated in their neighborhoods, and from black ministers who feared a loss of congregants to Catholicism.

In all, Katherine Drexel contributed to Native American and African-American missions of the Catholic Church in some thirty six states. As befit an investment banker's daughter, Drexel had a great command of finances, and carefully analyzed where to spend her money, scrutinizing the propriety of the actual expenditures. She missed very little, including details down to the level of pursuing rebates from railroads on freight charges for shipments made to her New Mexico missions.

In what was perhaps her signature achievement, Katherine Drexel began Xavier University in New Orleans, which started as a high school in 1915, but became the first Catholic college for African-Americans in 1925. At the time of Drexel's death, Xavier had 1100 students, and is today an integrated and coeducational university. Drexel also supported legislation and other efforts to assist African-Americans. Her work in this area included funding an NAACP investigation into racism in the South, and organizing support for federal anti-lynching legislation.

Katherine Drexel was a nun for sixty four years, during which time she spent $20 million dollars of her inheritance conducting her ministry. She suffered a heart attack in 1935 and retired in 1937, becoming a contemplative for the remaining eighteen years of her life. At the time of her death in 1955, the Blessed Sacrament sisters had fifty one convents with 501 sisters, and operated sixty one schools and one university.

Edward F. Mannino

MARY SCULLION

In 2009, *Time* Magazine named Mary Scullion one of "The World's Most Influential People," in recognition of her work with the homeless and mentally ill. A fierce and committed advocate for the poor, Scullion is the daughter of an Irish immigrant family living in Philadelphia, Pennsylvania. She attended Catholic grammar schools in northeast Philadelphia and Little Flower High School in the same city, where she worked with the Sisters of Mercy at a camp for inner-city children during the summer. She became a Sister of Mercy in 1974. Like most nuns today, Sister Mary is well-educated, with a Bachelor's degree in Psychology from St. Joseph's University, and a Masters in Social Work from Temple University.

Scullion's interest in working with the homeless was energized by her work at the 41st Eucharistic Congress, which was held in Philadelphia in 1975. There she was asked to help with Hunger for Bread Day, in the course of which she met several noted clerics, as well as Mother Teresa and Dorothy Day. She was motivated by liberation theologian Jon Sobrino, who said that "our work as Christians is to take Jesus off the cross." Scullion believes that we find Jesus on the cross today "in the suffering of people who are homeless, abused or subject to violence, in those who have addictions."

Scullion began her ministry with the homeless and mentally ill in 1978, and helped start a hospice home which was run by the Mercy order. She is most known for her work with Project H.O.M.E., which she and Joan Dawson McConnon, a Catholic layperson and accountant, started in 1989. Project H.O.M.E. provides housing, employment, education, and healthcare to the chronically homeless and poor. Its mission is "rooted in our strong spiritual conviction of the dignity of each person," and its stated vision is that "None of Us are Home Until All of Us are Home."

Scullion has shown a remarkable ability to raise funds for her efforts from both private and public sources, Catholic and non-Catholic. Religious orders, including the Sisters of Mercy, the Dominicans, and the Franciscans have contributed more than six million dollars to her efforts, particularly in the area of constructing or rehabilitating permanent housing for the homeless. The funding supplied by those orders has been complemented by individual and corporate donations, both large and small. Members of the Honickman family, who are Jewish, have contributed millions of dollars to set up a learning center, while Comcast Corporation has funded a technology lab, both of which are utilized to train the homeless and unemployed. Individual donors include the rock star Jon Bon Jovi, who has been very visible in supporting the efforts of Project H.O.M.E.

Project H.O.M.E. provides both housing and employment opportunities for the homeless, the poor, the addicted, and the mentally ill. In addition to providing housing, it has opened a bookstore, a café, and a used clothing store, all of which are staffed by residents or the unemployed. The efforts undertaken by Scullion and McConnon reduced the homeless population of Philadelphia from 2000 in 1989 to 200 in 2010, which has resulted in Philadelphia having the lowest per capita homeless population of any city in the world at that time.

The work of Project H.O.M.E. has helped over 8000 people. Remarkably, ninety five percent of them have not returned to the streets. It has developed close to 500 individual units of housing at twelve locations throughout Philadelphia. In 2009 alone, it provided services to some 500 individuals and families. Future plans include developing a Wellness Center for community-based holistic healthcare in partnership with Thomas Jefferson University Hospital.

In reviewing the work of Project H.O.M.E., United States Senator Robert Casey of Pennsylvania has rightly observed that Scullion and McConnon combine "soaring dreams and tough-minded practicality." Such can also be said for the marvelous work performed by thousands of other American nuns from the turn of the 18th century through today, of whom the four profiled above are a small sample. By helping the helpless, American nuns have served as a prime example of how Catholics have assisted in developing a conscience which illuminates all of American society.

CONCLUSION

THE CHANGING VIEW OF

AMERICAN CATHOLICS

Catholics have come a long way in the United States since Minister Cumings denounced "the Scarlet Whore...DRUNK WITH THE WINE OF HER FORNICATIONS" back in 1776. At that time, and continuing through the eighteenth and nineteenth centuries, American Catholics were viewed with suspicion, distrust, and sometimes outright hostility by American Protestants. That attitude spilled over into the twentieth century, reaching a particularly vicious zenith in the opposition to the candidacy of Alfred E. Smith, the Catholic Governor of New York, for the American presidency in 1928.

This negative view of American Catholics gradually changed, particularly after World War II. The animus toward Catholics which we treated at length in the Prologue is now quarantined to some fundamentalist Protestant congregations, joined by a relatively small contingent of college and law professors and several in the media. Non-Catholic Americans, by contrast, generally see their every fourth neighbor now as an integral part of the American tapestry. In this Conclusion, we demonstrate this change of attitude through a brief review of popular culture as manifested in Hollywood movies and popular television programs.

CATHOLIC PRIESTS AS HEROES IN AMERICAN MOVIES:
FROM FATHER FLANAGAN TO WAR HEROES TO LABOR PRIESTS

With Catholics as the moving force in the adoption of a Motion Picture Production Code in the 1930s, the portrayal of Catholic priests became more common in mainstream movies. Indeed, in stark contrast to the sex-crazed, murderous priests depicted in the 1839 best-seller, *Maria Monk's Awful Disclosures*, Hollywood's priests of the mid twentieth century were American heroes and figures to emulate. The movies discussed below represent a sample to illustrate this point.

We begin with "Boys Town" (1938), the movie based on a real-life priest, Father Edward Flanagan, who founded a home for wayward boys in Omaha, Nebraska. As the historian Christopher Shannon has pointed out, the movie portrays Flanagan first and foremost as an American, and only secondarily as a Catholic and a priest. The movie is overwhelmingly ecumenical; the boys belong to all religions, and much of Flanagan's financial support for Boys Town is supplied by individuals of other faiths. In addition, in the midst of the Great Depression and the Second New Deal, Boys Town illustrates what a better society would look like. There is no racism or discrimination in Boys Town, blacks and whites live together with no segregation, and a disabled ethnic boy can run for mayor. The priest is also a spiritual healer and hero. The movie begins with his hearing the confession of a convicted murderer on death row, who repents after his visit from Flanagan.

The theme of the Catholic priest as an American hero continued in "The Fighting 69th" (1940). Again, a real-life priest, Father Francis Duffy, provides the storyline. Duffy was the chaplain in World War I for the New York National Guard 69th Regiment, a largely Irish Catholic military unit which has been famous from the days of the Civil War for its bravery in battle. One battalion of the Regiment was headed by Major William "Wild Bill" Donovan, who won two Purple Hearts, the Distinguished Service Cross and the Medal of Honor for his heroism in World War I. Donovan went on to become the first Director of the Office of Strategic Services, which would morph into the Central Intelligence Agency, and was also the founder of a prominent New York law firm which bore his name. The Catholic regiment is portrayed in an ecumenical context, with Catholics depicted not as outsiders, but as an integral part of the American forces fighting to preserve American values in a war. One of its members, who was an aide to Donovan and died in battle, was the Catholic poet Joyce Kilmer, best remembered for the often imitated and sometimes ridiculed poem, "Trees." In the film, Father Duffy is portrayed as a model citizen, as befits reality, since he was the most decorated chaplain in American military history. His statue stands today in Times Square in New York.

In "On the Waterfront" (1954), the Catholic priest becomes the powerful defender of American workers. Once again, the movie is based upon an actual priest, the Jesuit Father John Corridan, one of the famous labor priests from that era. In urging the dockworkers of New York to fight the corrupt figures who control the New York waterfront, the movie's "Father Barry," played by Karl Malden, gives the most famous speech made by a priest in movie history.

Malden tells the dock workers, in a speech based on actual sermons delivered by Corridan, that "Christ is always with you — Christ is in the shape up. He's in the hatch. He's in the union hall. He's kneeling right here beside Dugan. Any he's saying with all of you, if you do it to the least of mine, you do it to me!" He also invokes Christian imagery in what has become known as the "Sermon on the Docks." Malden/Barry tells the workers that "Some people think the Crucifixion only took place on Calvary. They better wise up. Takin' Joey Doyle's life to stop him from testifying is a crucifixion. And dropping a sling on Kayo Dugan because he was ready to spill his guts tomorrow — that's a crucifixion. And every time the mob puts the crusher on a good man — tries to stop him from doing his duty as a citizen — it's a crucifixion. And anybody who sits around and lets it happen — keeps silent about something he knows has happened - shares the guilt of it just as much as the Roman soldier who pierced the flesh of Our Lord to see if He was dead."

BING CROSBY: THE CATHOLIC PRIEST AS REGULAR AMERICAN

As World War II came to an end, movies began to move away from the priest-reformer and hero to the priest as regular guy in a Roman collar. While movies like "On the Waterfront" continued the hero theme, Father Barry was a secondary figure in that film. The films which featured priests as lead characters put them in more mundane surroundings than Boys Town, the trenches of France in World War I, or the docks on New York's waterfront. Catholic priests became more mainline when Bing Crosby, then a major star as both singer and actor, portrayed Father Chuck O'Malley in two films made in the 1940s. In "Going My Way" (1944), and "The Bells of St. Mary's" (1945), Crosby played a priest who confronts and solves normal American financial difficulties for two different parishes, and his religion is presented in sympathetic terms. American nuns also come off well, with Ingrid Bergman portraying Sister Dominic in "The Bells of St. Mary's" as a tough-minded and admirable figure.

"Going My Way" was the top box office hit of 1944, and won seven Academy Awards, including the one for best picture, Crosby for best actor, and Barry Fitzgerald for best supporting actor in his role as the parish pastor, Father Fitzgibbon. Crosby's priest is a uniter who uses his talents to turn St. Dominic's parish around, reaching out to young gang members, to a young woman suspected of prostitution, and even to the elderly pastor whom he is secretly sent to effectively replace.

Father O'Malley accepts every one, explaining that "Going My Way" involves his following the more joyous parts of his religion, and encouraging others to do the same. He is not an ascetic cleric, but rather a former jazz musician and red-blooded American who can play stickball with the young men of the parish. He even convinces the young men to join the choir, which they resist at first, seeing it as too girlish. His manliness is further revealed when we meet his former girl friend, Jenny Linden, who is now a successful actress and singer, performing the lead role in "Carmen" at New York's Metropolitan Opera. (In an example of art imitating life, Linden is played by opera star Rise Stevens.) Linden helpfully assists O'Malley in solving the parish's financial problems by arranging an audition at the Metropolitan Opera at which St. Dominic's Choir will sing "Going My Way." The Met's representative does not like the song, but is impressed instead by the choir's performance of "Swinging on a Star," and buys the rights to perform it, thereby generating funds sufficient to repay the mortgage on the church.

"Going My Way" is a happy movie with a low-key Catholic communitarian vision, and Crosby's Irish-American charm is a major contributor to its success. Its underlying message is that all problems (including by inference the economic storms caused by Great Depression and World War II) can be solved with American ingenuity, if we all pull together. The Catholic characters are part of an American community now, not strange foreigners with stranger religious rites, and the Catholic religion is presented in a very subdued and relaxed form. Anthony Burke Smith has described Father O'Malley as a "very border-crossing character," and that portrayal, performed perfectly by a multimedia box office star and popular singer, continued the cultural integration of American Catholics into the surrounding Protestant society, which began to lower its borders to let them in.

CATHOLIC CHARACTERS ON AMERICAN TELEVISION

Catholic characters have also found starring roles in American television series. One such series was the "Father Dowling Mysteries" (1989-1991), which employed the priest-nun combination found in movies such as "The Bells of St. Mary's." Father Frank Dowling was a parish priest in Chicago who stumbled across murders and other crimes, solving them with the assistance of Sister Stephanie Oskowski, a street-wise nun with a checkered background of her own. Dowling is portrayed sympathetically as a kind and compassionate man, with very human habits and mannerisms. The series ran for three years, with some forty three episodes and one television movie. Father Dowling was played by Tom Bosley, a fatherly figure best remembered for playing Richie Cunningham's father on "Happy Days." The series was based on novels written by Ralph McInery, a Catholic philosopher who chaired the Department of Philosophy at the University of Notre Dame, and wrote twenty nine novels based on the Father Dowling character, as well as many books on philosophy and other novels, written under various pen names.

While the heroes in the early Hollywood movies included not only priest and nuns, but sometimes criminals as well, a number of American television programs in the twenty-first century chose instead to feature Catholic law enforcement professionals who are portrayed in positive terms, with their religion prominently noted. Perhaps the most notable is "Blue Bloods" (2010- present), which portrays the Reagan family of New York, with three generations who have served in New York Police Department or the justice system. Frank Reagan (played by Tom Selleck) is the incumbent police commissioner of New York, a position that was also held by his father Henry, before him. Three of Frank's sons — one of whom was murdered by a corrupt police officer while the young Reagan was working undercover — have also served as policemen or detectives, including one who just graduated from Harvard Law School. Frank's daughter, Erin, the divorced mother of a teenage girl, is a New York assistant district attorney. For the Reagans, the law is portrayed as a serious vocation, and one to which each of them is thoroughly committed.

"Blue Bloods" is suffused with Catholic imagery. The Reagans are portrayed as practicing Catholics, and their Sunday family dinner which is featured in every program always begins with grace being said. Priests come in and out of the programs as family friends, particularly of Commissioner Reagan, and the commissioner refuses to play by political rules of convenience. He adheres instead to a strict moral code, which bends only in such instances as where he urges a detective to look again into the case of the son of his cleaning woman at work, who turns out to have been unjustly accused of a crime.

In a particularly relevant episode, an old mob enemy named Whitey Brennan, who is dying, orders a hit on Commissioner Reagan. While Reagan is seriously wounded, he recovers, and the program ends with Reagan bringing a priest friend to the deathbed of the mob boss, encouraging him to make a full confession of his crimes and receive absolution before he dies.

The American Catholic family is also the focus of "American Dreams" (2002-2005). Set in Philadelphia in the 1960s, the series ran for sixty one episodes telling the story of the Catholic Pryor family, whose members experience all the turmoil and upheaval of that decade. The father, Jack Pryor, a former serviceman, owns a television and radio store, which he runs with the assistance of an African-American employee named Henry Walker. Jack eventually makes Henry a part owner, and goes on to win a City Council seat, which ends up with Jack taking a bribe to pay off the gambling debts of his son, J.J. Jack redeems himself by voting against his party to confirm an activist black minister for a seat on the Police Review Board. Jack is portrayed as a loving but strict father, and a traditional 1950s husband, who does not understand his wife's 1960s interest in working or going to college.

Helen Pryor, Jack's wife, is a housewife who longs to better herself intellectually. She eventually takes a job at a travel agency where she befriends a fellow employee who turns out to be gay, and is fired because of his sexual orientation. Helen also becomes active in a Catholic peace group which aids draft resisters during the Vietnam War.

Meg Pryor, the second child, is the protagonist and center of the series. She starts as a fairly vapid teenager who wins a spot as a regular dancer on the television show "Bandstand," but goes on to anti-war activities, getting arrested in a college protest with her friend, Sam Walker, an African-American scholarship student at the University of Pennsylvania, who is also Henry's son. There are suggestions of a romantic, interracial relationship, but as the series ends, Meg leaves Philadelphia with another anti-war activist, to go to California to further protest the Vietnam War.

Catholic imagery and settings predominate in "American Dreams." The children go to Catholic schools and East Catholic High School is a recurrent venue for the show, with multiple priests and nuns appearing throughout the series. Moral issues relating to race, war, gay rights, drugs, alcohol, gambling, and politics surface repeatedly, and the strain of such issues takes its toll on all the family members. They confront a new American reality which threatens their traditional American Dreams. In confronting this reality, their Catholic faith provides an implicit guide for their decision-making.

In these depictions of lay people, both practicing and nonpracticing Catholics, the characters are portrayed favorably as fellow Americans who experience the moral challenges of contemporary society and do their imperfect best to stand up for what they each perceive to be right.

THE DARKER SIDE

While the the American public at large now generally accepts Catholics as part of the mainstream, pockets of prejudice still exist. We have previously described how academics and cartoonists have attacked Catholic members of the Supreme Court of the United States for upholding a federal law banning partial-birth abortion by linking that decision to the justices' religion and questioning whether Catholics should even sit to decide cases involving issues on which the Catholic Church has taken a strong position. Unfortunately, this more or less random prejudice is likely to be fueled and to spread further as a result of the widespread media coverage of the late twentieth century priest abuse scandal, which threatens to resurface the old *Maria Monk* view of priests as sexual predators, albeit with children, rather than nuns, as their new victims.

Indeed, there are a few fundamentalist Protestant congregations who still assail Catholics with the same vehemence as Minister Cumings did in 1776. A particularly notable current example is provided by the Westboro Baptist Church, a small group of mainly family members who have picketed some 600, mostly military, funerals over a twenty year period, contending that God is punishing the United States for condoning homosexuality and divorce. The Westboro group has made a particular target of the Catholic Church, focusing on the priest abuse crisis, but going beyond that legitimate target to make a more general and fundamental attack.

The activities of the Westboro group came before the Supreme Court of the United States in the case of *Snyder v. Phelps* (2011), where the Chief Justice of the United States, John Roberts, himself a Catholic, wrote the majority opinion reversing a multimillion dollar judgment against members of the church. The Supreme Court ruled, by an eight to one margin, that the church members had a right under the First Amendment to the Constitution to picket the funeral of a Catholic Marine, Matthew Snyder, who was killed in Iraq. At a legally prescribed distance from the site of the funeral, members of the church held up signs stating "Pope in Hell" and "Priests Rape Boys." In addition, anti-Catholic comments were posted online by members of the church. These comments included attacks directed at Mathew's divorced parents, including that they purportedly taught Matthew "to defy his Creator, and to divorce, and to commit adultery. They taught him how to support the largest pedophile machine in the history of the entire world, the Roman Catholic monstrosity. Every dime they gave the Roman Catholic monster they condemned their own souls. They also, in supporting satanic Catholicism, taught Matthew to be an idolator."

The Westboro "church" and their academic and media colleagues show that the pestilence of anti-Catholicism, like the plague in Albert Camus' novel, still lies dormant beneath the surface, despite the efforts of Americans of all faiths and of no faith at all, to bury it once and for all. As Camus put it, "the plague bacillus never dies or disappears for good" and the day may come when it can "rouse up its rats again and send them forth to die in [our] happy city."

ENDNOTES

PROLOGUE:

THE CATHOLIC CONSCIENCE IN AMERICAN HISTORY

The quotation at the head of the Prologue appears in Thomas S. Kidd, *God of Liberty: A Religious History of the American Revolution* (New York: Basic Books, 2010), 72.

The genesis of anti-Catholic feeling in America arising from the Seven Years War and the reigns of Charles II and James II is well traced in Kidd, *God of Liberty,* at 16-20, 25, 29-31, 40-41, and 58-72.

Accounts of the Philadelphia Bible Riots of 1844 are given in Charles R. Morris, *American Catholic: The Saints and Sinners Who Built America's Most Powerful Church* (New York: Vintage Books, 1998), 60-61 , and in Kenneth C. Davis, *A Nation Rising* (New York: HarperCollins, 2010), 185-194. For a more general discussion of the American Bible Wars in the nineteenth century, see Denis Lacorne, *Religion in America: A Political History* (New York: Columbia University Press, 2011), 69-78.

For accounts of the 1834 burning of the Ursuline convent in Charlestown, Massachusetts, and the "Maria Monk" book, see Morris, *American Catholic*, at 54-60, and Mark S. Massa, *Anti-Catholicism in America: The Last Acceptable Prejudice* (New York: Crossroad Publishing Company, 2003), 24-26.

The Hamilton comment on the Quebec Act is quoted in Kidd, *God of Liberty*, at 69. John Jay's comment is quoted in *First Things*, April 2012, at 67. The Sam Adams comment on "Popery" appears in Kidd, *God of Liberty*, at 58.

The Adams-Jefferson letter is quoted in John T. Mc Greevy, *Catholicism and American Freedom: A History* (New York: W. W. Norton & Company, 2003), 33.

The quotation from the Free Soiler on "freedom, temperance and Protestantism" is reported in Morton Keller, *America's Three Regimes: A New Political History* (New York: Oxford University Press 2007), 118.

The quotation from Abraham Lincoln on the Know Nothings is

reported in Robert V. Remini, *A Short History of the United States* (New York: HarperCollins Publishers, 2008), 137.

The quotation from Ralph Waldo Emerson on the "Roman Church" is reported in McGreevy, *Catholicism and American Freedom*, at 88.

The quotation from Elizabeth Cady Stanton on the Catholic idea of authority is reported in McGreevy, *Catholicism and American Freedom*, at 95.

The "priestcraft" quotation from President Grant was made in his final annual Address to Congress, and is recorded at 4 Congressional Record 175 (1875). The other quotations in the text from President Grant and James A. Garfield are reported in McGreevy, *Catholicism and American Freedom*, at 91, 92, and 93.

The comments from the Senate debates on the Blaine amendment are reported in Meir Katz, "The State of Blaine: A Closer Look at the Blaine Amendments and Their Modern Application," *Engage*, Volume 12, Issue 1, 111, at 112 (June 2011).

The fourth Oath of the American Protective Association quoted in the text is reported in Katz, "The State of Blaine," at 118, n. 15.

The quotations from Walter Rauschenbusch are found in *Christianity and the Social Crisis in the 21st Century*, ed. Paul Rauschenbusch (New York: HarperCollins Publishers, 2007), 158, 169.

ORESTES BROWNSON CRITIQUES THE AMERICAN REPUBLIC

For a short biography of Orestes Brownson, see 3 *American National Biography*, general eds., John A. Garraty and Mark C. Carnes (New York: Oxford University Press, 1999), 777-778. See also McGreevy, *Catholicism and American Freedom*, at 42-49, 66-68, 75-77, 79-81, and 88-90; Arthur M. Schlesinger, Jr., *Orsetes Brownson: A Pilgrim's Progress* (New York: Octagon Books, 1963) (originally published 1939).

The quotation in the text from Cardinal Newman regarding Brownson being America's greatest thinker appears in the Introduction to the 2003 edition of Orestes Brownson, *The American Republic: Its Constitution, Tendencies, and Destiny* (Washington, D.C.: Regnery Publishing, Inc., 2003) (originally published 1865), xiii .

The quotation in the text from Brownson regarding the people collectively constituting society appears in *The American Republic*, at 39.

The quotations in the text from Brownson regarding the place of Catholics in the United States appear in *The American Republic*, at xxx and 182.

The quotations in the text from Brownson regarding the mission of the United States and the twin problems of individualism and humanitarianism appear in *The American Republic*, at 4-5,178, 43,170, 172, and 187 respectively.

DEFENSE OF THE LABORER IN THE GILDED AGE

For an overview of the state of American labor and the labor strikes mentioned in the text, see Edward F. Mannino, *Shaping America: The Supreme Court and American Society* (Columbia, S.C.: University of South Carolina Press, 2009), 78-81.

For a vivid recreation of the sights and sounds of the Great Railroad Strike of 1877, see Cecelia Holland, *Blood on the Tracks* (2011), an electronic book available at www.amazon.com/kindlesingles .

The excerpts from Justice Miller's 1888 commencement address at the University of Iowa are reprinted in Michael A. Ross, *Justice of Shattered Dreams: Samuel Freeman Miller and the Supreme Court during the Civil War Era* (Baton Rouge, LA: Louisiana State University Press, 2003), 242-243.

The quotation from George Baer is referenced in II Samuel Eliot Morison and Henry Steele Commager, *The Growth of the American Republic* (New York: Oxford University Press, 1950), 164.

On Cardinal Gibbons, see the entries in 8 *American National Biography*, at 909-910, and *The Encyclopedia of American Catholic History*, eds. Michael Glazier and Thomas J. Shelley (Collegeville, MN: The Liturgical Press, 1997), 584-588.

The "soiled hands" and "humble child" quotations in the text from Cardinal Gibbons are referenced in Larry Witham, *A City Upon a Hill: How Sermons Changed the Course of American History* (New York: HarperOne 2007), 182, 185. The quotations in the text from Gibbons' submission to the Vatican on the Knights of Labor are from his February 20, 1887 Defense of the Knights of Labor, reproduced in *Documents of American Catholic History*, ed. John Tracy Ellis (Milwaukee, WI: Bruce Publishing Company, 1956), 460, 463-464, 468.

On Archbishop Ireland, see 11 *American National Biography*, at 675-677, and *Catholic History Encyclopedia*, at 687-693.

Edward F. Mannino

Opposition to Eugenics

Law professor Victoria Nourse reports that more than 375 colleges and universities offered eugenics classes, and is the source for the 20,000 student attendance estimate. See Victoria F. Nourse, *In Reckless Hands: Skinner v. Oklahoma and the Near Triumph of American Eugenics* (New York: W.W. Norton & Company, Inc., 2008), 20. Nourse also reports the enactment of new sterilization laws in twelve states in the two years following the Supreme Court decision. Nourse, *Reckless Hands*, at 31.

William Shockley's position on voluntary sterilization of those with low IQs and his 1974 television interview statements on African American intelligence are reported in Bobby White, "Donor's Views on Race Spark Outcry Over Parkland," *The Wall Street Journal*, August 31, 2009, A4.

For the quotation from Archbishop Shaw and a helpful general discussion of Catholic opposition to eugenics, see McGreevy, *Catholicism and American Freedom*, at 223-225. Nourse, *Reckless Hands*, at 21, 30, and 56, also notes the Catholic opposition to eugenics.

Catholics, the Great Depression, and the New Deal

The full text of President Franklin Delano Roosevelt's first Inaugural Address appears in *The Inaugural Addresses of the Presidents* (New York: Gramercy Press, 1995), 377-382. The quotations in the text appear at 378-379.

For a discussion of the reaction of the Catholic intellectual community to Roosevelt and his New Deal, see Anthony Burke Smith, *The Look of Catholics: Portrayals in Popular Culture from the Great Depression to the Cold War* (Lawrence, KS: University Press of Kansas, 2010), 19-23. The quotation in the text from *America* appears in Smith, *The Look of Catholics*, at 20.

On Father Coughlin, see 5 *American National Biography*, at 578-581; *Catholic History Encyclopedia*, at 385-387; and Michael Kazin, *The Populist Persuasion: An American History* (Ithaca, NY: Cornell University Press, revised ed., 1998), 109-133.

On Monsignor Ryan, see 19 *American National Biography*, at 145-146; *Catholic History Encyclopedia*, at 1226-1230; and Chapter 3 of Charles E. Curran, *Catholic Moral Theology in the United States:*

A History (Washington, D.C.: Georgetown University Press, 2008). For the text of the 1919 *Bishops' Program of Social Reconstruction*, see Ellis, *Catholic Documents*, at 611-629.

On Dorothy Day, see 6 *American National Biography*, at 265-267; *Catholic History Encyclopedia*, at 413-417; Mark S. Massa, *Catholics and American Culture: Fulton Sheen, Dorothy Day, and the Notre Dame Football Team* (New York: Crossroad Publishing Company, 1999), 102-127; Paul Elie, *The Life You Save May Be Your Own: An American Pilgrimage* (New York: Farrar, Straus and Giroux, 2003); and Robert Ellsberg, "Remembering Dorothy Day," http://www.huffingtonpost.com, (accessed July 21, 2011). The quotations from Day regarding the Catholic Church as the church of the poor, the Catholic Church's social program, and the need for poverty to be decent are referenced in Massa, *Catholics and American* Culture, at 104, 105, and 116. The most influential person quotation from *Commonweal* is referenced in Morris, *American Catholic*, at 141.

COMMUNISM, THE COLD WAR, AND RACIAL SEGREGATION

The cartoon from *The Tablet* referenced in the text is reprinted in Morris, *American Catholic*, at 235.

For a fuller discussion of the impact of the Cold War on both anti-Communism and racial segregation, see Mannino, *Shaping America*, at 135-141, 196-197.

On Archbishop Ireland's opposition to segregation, see McGreevy, *Catholicism and American Freedom*, at 120.

For biographical sketches of Father John LaFarge, see *Catholic History Encyclopedia*, at 789-791, and 13 *American National Biography*, at 30-31.

PART II

CHAPTER I – THE GRACE-FILLED WORLD OF FLANNERY O'CONNOR

The quotation from Flannery O'Connor which appears at the head of the chapter is quoted in Lorraine V. Murray, *The Abbess of*

Edward F. Mannino

Andalusia: Flannery O'Connor's Spiritual Journey (Charlotte, NC: Saint Benedict Press, 2009), 110.

The full quotation from Thomas Merton comparing O'Connor to Sophocles appears in Thomas Merton, *Raids on the Unspeakable* (New York: New Directions Publ. Co., 1966), 42.

O'Connor's June 16, 1962 letter to Alfred Corn appears in *The Habit of Being: Letters of Flannery O'Connor*, ed. Sally Fitzgerald (New York: Vintage Books, 1980), 479.

The quotation about the action of grace on a character appears in *Flannery O'Connor: Spiritual Writings* , ed., Robert Ellsberg (Maryknoll, NY,: Orbis Books, 2005), 16.

The quotation about stories as guides appears in Flannery O'Connor's 1963 Georgetown speech, "The Catholic Novelist in the Protestant South," and is reprinted in *Flannery O'Connor: Collected Works* (New York: The Library of America, 1988), 853-864.

THE SICK AND DISABLED: "TEMPLES OF THE HOLY GHOST"

The quotations on sickness as one of God's mercies and on sickness as a place both appear in *Spiritual Writings*, at 24.

"A Temple of the Holy Ghost" is reprinted in *Collected Works*, at 197-209. The story is helpfully discussed in Richard Giannone, *Flannery O'Connor: Hermit Novelist* (Urbana, IL: University of Illinois Press, 2000), 98-103, and Ralph G. Wood, *Flannery O'Connor and the Christ-Haunted South* (Grand Rapids, MI: William B. Eerdmans Publishing Company, 2004), 244-248. O'Connor's 1954 letter on the story quoted in the text is reprinted in *Collected Works*, at 925.

CHRISTIAN ATHEISTS: THE GRANDMOTHER AND THE MISFIT

For the concept of "Christian atheists," see Wood, at 38-39, who traces it to John Wesley. Interestingly, the young boy in "A Good Man Is Hard to Find," is named John Wesley.

For O'Connor's self-reference as a "hillbilly Thomist," see *Spiritual Writings*, at 49.

The quotation about writing for the hard of hearing and almost-blind is cited in Richard Giannone, "Flannery O'Connor's Dialogue with the Age," in *Spiritual Writings*, at 18.

"A Good Man Is Hard to Find" is reprinted in *Collected Works*, at 137-153.

The quotation in the text referring to "repulsive" Catholics who embrace religion as the "poor man's insurance system" appears in a letter to Cecil Dawkins dated July 16, 1957, reprinted in *Habit of Being*, at 230-231. The quotation about faith as a big electric blanket appears in *Spiritual Writings*, at 48.

The parable of the Pharisee and the tax collector is told in Luke 18: 9-14.

The quotation regarding the grandmother's "superficial beliefs" appears in a letter to a "Professor of English" dated March 28, 1961, reprinted in *Habit of Being*, at 437.

Richard Giannone's analysis of "A Good Man Is Hard to Find" appears in Giannone, at 103-110.

EPIPHANIES: RUBY TURPIN'S "REVELATION"

The quotations in the text about the grandmother's gesture and its impact on The Misfit appear in *Spiritual Writings*, at 134-135, n.*.

"Revelation" is reprinted in *Collected Works,* at 633-654. For an excellent discussion of the story, relating its messages to those of the Desert Fathers, see Giannone, at 226-235. See also Wood, at 261-264.

O'Connor's letter to Maryat Lee is reprinted in *Collected Works*, at 1207-1208.

For a brief discussion of sanctifying grace and the Council of Trent, see *The HarperCollins Encyclopedia of Catholicism*, ed., Richard P. McBrien (New York: HarperCollins, 1995), 583-584.

CHAPTER 2 – THOMAS MERTON: AMERICA'S SPIRITUAL DIRECTOR

Merton's Obituary by Israel Shenker appears in the December 11, 1968 *New York Times* on page 1, under the title, "Thomas Merton Is Dead at 53; Monk Wrote of Search for God."

MERTON'S LIFE AND WORK

The authorized biography of Merton is Michael Mott, *The Seven Mountains of Thomas Merton* (Boston: Houghton Mifflin Co., 1984). More insightful biographies are those by Lawrence S. Cunningham, *Thomas Merton and the Monastic Vision* (Grand Rapids, MI: William D. Eerdmans Publ. Co., 1999) and Monica Furlong, *Merton: A Biography* (Liguori, MO: Liguori Publications, 1995) (New Edition). Merton's life is also admirably covered in Paul Elie, *The Life You Save*.

The International Thomas Merton Society, headquartered at the Thomas Merton Center of Bellarmine University in Louisville, Kentucky, publishes articles by and about Merton, and an ongoing bibliography of works by and about Merton, in both *The Merton Annual*, and in *The Merton Seasonal: A Quarterly Review*. The Society has a website at http://www.merton.org/ITMS/.

Much of Merton's work began as meditations done in his Journals, which have been published in several volumes. A good selection of his Journal entries is *The Intimate Merton: His Life from His Journals*, eds., Patrick Hart and Jonathan Montaldo (New York: HarperSanFrancisco, 2001) (paperback ed.)

Merton's poems appear in numerous editions. The best collection is *In The Darkness Before Dawn: New Selected Poems of Thomas Merton*, ed. Lynn R. Szabo (New York: New Directions Publ. Corp., 2005). "Chants..." appears at pages 119-122. "Original Child Bomb" appears at pages 111-118.

A good selection of Merton's letters appears in *Thomas Merton: A Life in Letters: The Essential Collection*, eds., Wiliam H. Shannon and Christine M. Bochen (New York: HarperCollins Publishers, 2008).

Merton's Cold War Letters are collected in Thomas Merton, *Cold War Letters* (Maryknoll, NY: Orbis Books, 2006).

The suicide as "demonic" comment is recounted in Elie, *The Life You Save*, at 378.

Merton's literary essays are collected in *The Literary Essays of Thomas Merton*, ed. Brother Patrick Hart (New York: New Directions Publ. Corp., 1995) (paperback ed.)

The quotation about "the Christ of the burnt men" appears in Thomas Merton, *The Seven Storey Mountain: An Autobiography of Faith* (Orlando, FL: Harcourt, Inc., 1998) (Fiftieth Anniversary Edition), 462.

MERTON'S WRITINGS ON CONTEMPLATION AND THE TRUE AND FALSE SELF

The quotation from Merton about the illusion of "separation from the world" appears in his meditation on the Fourth and Walnut experience in his *Conjectures of a Guilty Bystander* (New York: Doubleday, 1989) (paperback ed.), 157. The Fourth and Walnut experience is recounted at 156-158.

The quotation from Merton about the opposition of the transcendent and external selves appears in *New Seeds of Contemplation* (New York: New Directions Publ. Corp., 1972) (paperback ed.), 7.

The quotation from Merton about "some other poet, some other saint" appears in *New Seeds*, at 98.

The quotation from Merton about no two beings being exactly alike appears in *New Seeds*, at 29.

The quotation from Merton about alienation and masks appears in *The Literary Essays of Thomas Merton*, at 381.

The references by Merton to "evanescent shadow" and "smoke self" appear in *New Seeds*, at 279 and 38 respectively.

The quotation from Merton about escaping from the prison of our false self appears in Thomas Merton, *No Man Is An Island* (New York: Harvest Books, 1983), 25.

MERTON'S INCARNATIONAL SPIRITUALITY

The quotation from Merton on the "forms and characters of living and growing things" appears in *New Seeds*, at 30.

The excerpt from Merton's poem, "The Trappist Abbey: Matins," appears in *New Selected Poems*, at 26.

The excerpts from Merton's poem, "Elegy for a Trappist," appear in *New Selected Poems*, at 43-44.

THOMAS MERTON, FIRE WATCHER

Merton's "Fire Watcher" meditation appears in Thomas Merton, *The Sign of Jonas* (New York: Harcourt Brace, 1953), 350-362.

The quotations about Merton and the Fire Watcher appear in

William Harmless, S.J., *Mystics* (New York: Oxford University Press, 2008), 39-40.

Retreats and workshops based on Merton's writings are sponsored by the Merton Institute for Contemplative Living , which also has issued a series of booklets entitled "Bridges to Contemplative Living" published by Ave Maria Press in Notre Dame, Indiana. The Institute has a website at http://www.mertoninstitute.org.

CHAPTER 3 – FULTON J. SHEEN: AMERICA'S CATHOLIC TELEVANGELIST

SHEEN'S LIFE AND WORKS

The authoritative biography of Fulton Sheen, on which I have drawn extensively, is Thomas C. Reeves, *America's Bishop: The Life and Times of Fulton J. Sheen* (San Francisco: Encounter books, 2001). For short biographies, see *Catholic History Encyclopedia*, at 1285-1288 and 19 *American National Biography*, at 772-774.

Mark Massa has a helpful chapter on Sheen in his *Catholics and American Culture*, at 82-101, as does Anthony Burke Smith in his *The Look of Catholics*, at 125-151. Charles P. Connor's *The Spiritual Legacy of Archbishop Fulton J. Sheen* (Staten Island, NY: St. Pauls, 2010) has additional background on Sheen and quotes extensively from his books.

Sheen tells his own story in an autobiography published posthumously in 1980, and titled *Treasure in Clay* (San Francisco: Ignatius Press, 1993) (paperback reprint).

The London paper's reference to Sheen as "the American Chesterton" is referenced in Reeves, *America's Bishop*, at 81.

Sheen's use of the "faith depends on reason" quote is referenced in Reeves, *America's Bishop*, at 43.

For an account of the conversion of Clare Boothe Luce, see Reeves, *America's Bishop*, at 175-178.

Sheen's New York classes for converts are described in Connor, *Spiritual Legacy*, at 80. Connor recounts several conversions by Sheen at 76-83 and 98-101. Sheen describes his efforts at conversion, going over several specific cases, including Clare Booth Luce, in *Treasure in Clay*, at 251-279.

A picture of Sheen's house in Washington appears in "Memories of an Archbishop," *The Wall Street Journal*, March 23, 2007. The house is also discussed in Reeves, *America's Bishop*, at 121-123.

For Sheen's reading of communist periodicals, see Reeves, *America's Bishop*, at 127.

Sheen's opposition to Freudian psychoanalysis is documented in Reeves, *America's Bishop*, at 198-202.

Sheen's views of the New Deal and the Catholic Worker are discussed in Reeves, *America's Bishop*, at 90-91.

Sheen's views against racism, anti-Semitism and use of the atomic bomb are detailed in Reeves, *America's Bishop*, at 5, 161, 280-281. His opposition to the Vietnam War is covered in Reeves, at 6, 309, and 327.

Sheen's views on modern bible scholarship are set forth in Reeves, *America's Bishop*, at 257 and 268.

SHEEN'S MEDIA CAREER

For a detailed discussion of Sheen's work on The Catholic Hour, see Smith, *The Look of Catholics*, at 128-134. The subject is also discussed in Massa, *Catholics and American Culture*, at 89-90 and Reeves, *America's Bishop*, at 110.

For a discussion of Life Is Worth Living, see Massa, *Catholics and American Culture*, at 82-85 and 93-97, and Reeves, *America's Bishop*, at 223-241 and 255-256.

SHEEN'S SERVICE AND OFFICES IN THE CATHOLIC CHURCH

The $10,000,000 contribution figure for Sheen's charitable donations is given in Reeves, *America's Bishop*, at 4, based on an estimate made by Sheen in 1973.

The two disputes with Cardinal Spellman are detailed in Reeves, *America's Bishop*, at 252-255.

Sheen's service in Rochester is described in Reeves, *America's Bishop*, at 291-327

"LIFE IS WORTH LIVING": THOMISM FOR THE PEOPLE

44 of Sheen's recreated talks from Life Is Worth Living are

Edward F. Mannino

contained in Fulton J. Sheen, *Life Is Worth Living* (San Francisco: Ignatius Press, 1998) (paperback reprint)

"The Philosophy of Communism" appears in *Life Is Worth Living*, at 52-58. "Why Work Is Boring" appears in id., at 222-227. "Reparation" appears at 152-158, and "Pain and Suffering" appears at 131-138.

The text of President Eisenhower's Proclamation for a National Day of Penance and Prayer is set forth in *Life Is Worth Living*, at 158, n.1.

GOD'S HOUND: BRINGING FAITH THROUGH REASON

For Sheen's fondness for "The Hound of Heaven," and for Thompson's life story, see Connor, *Spiritual Legacy*, at 19-20.

CHAPTER 4 – BRUCE SPRINGSTEEN: THE SEARCH FOR FAITH AND MEANING IN A TROUBLED WORLD

The quotation from Father Andrew Greeley which appears at the head of this Chapter appears in his article "The Catholic Imagination of Bruce Springsteen," which was published in *America*, February 16, 1998, and reprinted in *Racing in the Street: The Bruce Springsteen Reader*, ed., June Skinner Sawyers (New York: Penguin Books, 2004) (paperback ed.), 159.

SPRINGSTEEN'S LIFE AND CAREER

Springsteen's recollection of the incident with the nun is quoted on the back cover of John Duffy, *Bruce Springsteen: In His Own Words* (London: Omnibus Press, 2003) (paperback ed.). His experience with the priest saying Mass is recounted in Rob Kirkpatrick, *Magic in the Night: The Words and Music of Bruce Springsteen* (New York: St. Martin's Griffin, 2009) (paperback ed.), 4

SPRINGSTEEN'S SPIRITUALITY

Springsteen's remark about quitting religion is quoted in Louis P. Masur, *Runaway Dream: Born to Run and Bruce Springsteen's American Vision* (New York: Bloomsbury Press, 2010) (paperback ed.), 20, and in *In His Own Words*, at 86.

The quotation in the text from Springsteen regarding the powerful world of Catholic imagery appears in *Runaway Dream*, at 177.

The quotation in the text from Springsteen about "Mary's Place" appears in Jeffrey B. Symynkywicz, *The Gospel according to Bruce Springsteen* (Louisville, KY: Westminster John Knox Press, 2008) (paperback ed.), 148.

Springsteen's remark that "once you're a Catholic, there's no getting out" can be heard on the VH1 Storyteller's Album, "Bruce Springsteen" (DVD 2005).

The quotations from Will Percy's interview with Springsteen appear in *Doubletake*, Volume 4, No.2, Spring 1998, respectively at 38, 40, 41, 42, and at 36, 37, 42, and 43.

SPRINGSTEEN'S SONGS

The quotation in the text from Andy Whitman appears in his article, "Bruce Springsteen and the Long Walk Home," *Image*, No. 66, Summer, 2010, 97, 100.

The "Christ-haunted" phrase is from the title of Ralph Wood's book on Flannery O'Connor.

The quotation from Father Greeley on "Catholic minstrels" appears in his *"Catholic Imagination"* article, at 164.

CHAPTER 5 – DENISE LEVERTOV AND JOHN BERRYMAN: THE POET'S RELIGIOUS IMAGINATION

The quotation from Denise Levertov which appears at the head of the chapter appears in her final interview, which may be found at www. english.illinois.edu/maps/poets under "Denise Levertov," "Levertov's Final Interview, A Poet's Valediction by Nicholas O'Connell."

DENISE LEVERTOV

Levertov's biography and career are helpfully covered in the Modern American Poetry website, accessible under "Denise Levertov" at www.english.illinois.edu/maps/poets (cited hereafter as "MAPS"). Excellent discussions of Levertov and her poetry are also found in The Poetry Foundation website, accessible under "Poems & Poets" "Denise Levertov" at www.poetryfoundation.org , and in Murray

Bodo, "Denise Levertov: A Memoir and Appreciation," *Image*, Issue 27, Summer 2000.

The view of the poet as having a "priestly" role is attributed to Levertov by Susan J. Zeuenberger in her entry on Levertov in the *Oxford Companion to Women's Writing in the United States*, eds., Cathy N. Davidson and Linda Wagner-Martin (New York: Oxford University Press, 1995). Zeuenberger's work is reprinted in the MAPS materials on Levertov under the entry "Denise Levertov's Life and Career."

The Stanford University Memorial Resolution for Levertov is accessible at www.stanford.edu at /dept/facultysenate/ archive/1997_1998/reports.

Joan F. Hallisey's view of Levertov's poetry as combining the mystical with a firm commitment to social issues appears in MAPS under "Themes in Denise Levertov's Poetry."

The quotations from Levertov's interviews appear in MAPS under "Levertov's Final Interview: A Poet's Valediction by Nicholas O'Connell" and "Levertov Interviewed by Sybil Estess." The observations about William Carlos Williams, her writing of "explicitly Christian poems," and poetry as "a form of prayer" all appear in the Final Interview. The comments about Wallace Stevens as "very musical" and writing poetry as a "religious experience" appear in the Estess interview.

The quotation from Levertov regarding William Carlos Williams' "Franciscan sense of wonder" appears in Bodo, *Denise Levertov Interview*.

Levertov's reference to her "slow development from agnosticism to Christian faith" appears in Denise Levertov, *The Stream & the Sapphire: Selected Poems on Religious Themes* (New York: New Directions Publishing Corp., 1997), vii.

THE STREAM & THE SAPPHIRE

All of the poems discussed in the text appear in *Stream & Sapphire*.

"The Servant-Girl at Emmaus" appears in *Stream & Sapphire*, at 43-44. The Velazquez painting which is the subject of the poem is not the more famous one which is at the Metropolitan Museum of Art in New York, but rather a 1617/18 painting which is in the collection of the National Gallery of Ireland in Dublin. A reproduction of the National Gallery painting may be seen in plate 1 of Tanya J. Tiffany, "Light, Darkness, and African Salvation: Velazquez's *Supper at Emmaus*," *Art History*, February 2008, at 33. It should be noted that Levertov takes some poetic liberty in her poem, since the servant girl in the National Gallery painting is not in the dining room with Christ and the disciples, but is from a later time and is pictured in a room in which the other, more famous, painting hangs on the wall.

"On a Theme from Julian's Chapter XX" appears in *Stream & Sapphire*, at 75-76.

"What the Figtree Said" appears in *Stream & Sapphire*, at 67-68.

"Agnus Dei"" appears in *Stream & Sapphire*, at 12-14.

JOHN BERRYMAN

A short biography of John Berryman appears in 2 *American National Biography,* at 690-692.

Denise Levertov's observation about poets having to spend "some time in a mental hospital" appears in the Final Interview.

"ELEVEN ADDRESSES TO THE LORD"

"Eleven Addresses to the Lord" appears in John Berryman, *Love & Fame* (New York: Farrar, Straus and Giroux, 1970), 85-96, and is reprinted in *American Religious Poems: An Anthology by Harold Bloom*, eds. Harold Bloom and Jesse Zuba (New York: Library of America, 2006), 334-340. Elizabeth Kirkland Cahill's "Tormented Witness: John Berryman's Addresses to God," *Commonweal*, July 15, 2011, at 12-13, provides a helpful commentary on the poems.

The quotations in the text from "Eleven Addresses" appear in *Love & Fame*, at 85, 91, 88, 93, 89, 96, and 86 respectively.

PART II

CHAPTER 6 – AL SMITH: THE CATHOLIC AS PROGRESSIVE

The best biography is Robert A. Slayton, *Empire Statesman: The Rise and Redemption of Al Smith* (New York: Free Press,

2001) (paperback ed.). For short biographies, see *Catholic History Encyclopedia*, at 1329-1334, and 20 *American National Biography*, at 129-133.

Smith penned an early autobiography, published as *Up to Now* (New York: Viking Press, 1929).

For an exhaustive recent treatment of Catholic social thought, see Michael P. Hornsby-Smith, *An Introduction to Catholic Social Thought* (Cambridge and New York: Cambridge University Press, 2006). The author provides a nice summary of key concepts at 104-107.

EARLY LIFE

For Smith's description of himself as an "F.F.M. man," see Slayton, *Empire Statesman*, at 32.

David Burner's "disorder of pets" description appears in his entry on Smith in *American National Biography*, at 132. For an account of the zoo at the Governor's Mansion, see Slayton, *Empire Statesman*, at 228-229.

POLITICAL CAREER

Smith's early difficulties with the legislative process are described in Slayton, *Empire Statesman*, at 72-73.

For Smith's use of "let's look at the record," see Slayton, *Empire Statesman*, at 107.

For his work on the Factory Investigating Committee, see Slayton, *Empire Statesman*, at 89-100.

Smith's political priorities are summarized in Slayton, *Empire Statesman*, at 101.

GOVERNOR AL SMITH

For Smith's margin of victory and support in the 1918 election, see Slayton, *Empire Statesman*, at 120-121.

For short biographies of Joseph Proskauer, see *The Yale Biographical Dictionary of American Law*, ed. Roger K. Newman (New Haven, CT: Yale University Press, 2009), 439, and 17 *American National Biography*, at 905-906.

Smith's vetoes as a first-term governor of the bills discussed in the text are reviewed in Slayton, *Empire Statesman*, at 135-139.

Presidential Campaigns

On the 1920 Democratic Convention, see Slayton, *Empire Statesman*, at 146-148.

For the Proskauer-Roosevelt controversy over "the happy warrior" speech at the 1924 Democratic Convention, see Slayton, *Empire Statesman*, at 209-210.

The Klan's "pope-loving governor" quote appears in Slayton, *Empire Statesman*, at 203.

On the articles in the *Atlantic Monthly*, see Slayton, *Empire Statesman*, at 302-304.

The anti-Catholic quotes in the text taken from Chapter 18 of Slayton, *Empire Statesman* appear at ix, 246-247, 308, 311-312. Some of the period cartoons are reproduced in Slayton, in a pictorial section appearing between pages 224 and 225.

Different portions of Smith's 1928 campaign Oklahoma City speech are reproduced in *Catholic History Encyclopedia*, at 1332-1334, and in Slayton, *Empire Statesman*, at xiv.

For the charge that the church had purchased high ground to train artillery on the federal government, see 20 *American National Biography*, at 132.

Smith's Career after Politics

For Smith's career after politics, see Slayton, *Empire Statesman*, at 331-362 and 376-402.

Smith's 1932 Jefferson Day speech is quoted in Amity Shlaes, *The Forgotten Man: A New History of the Great Depression* (New York: HarperCollins, 2007), 128.

The "baloney dollars" quotation in the text appears in Albert Fried, *FDR and His Enemies* (New York: Palgrave, 2001) (paperback ed.), 89.

Smith's view of the primacy of state government is described in Slayton, *Empire Statesman*, at 382.

Smith's denunciation of Hitler appears in Slayton, *Empire Statesman*, at 390, and his speech on white racism is noted at 391. Smith's work with African-Americans in New York is covered at 286-287.

SMITH'S CATHOLICISM

Smith's Catholic school education is described in Slayton, *Empire Statesman*, at 26-30. His daughter's view of the church as the "heart and center" of the parish and "an intimate part of our daily lives" is quoted at 27.

Smith's "good Catholic doctrine" quote appears in Slayton, *Empire Statesman*, at 96-97.

Smith's "Remember the Sabbath day" quote appears in Slayton, *Empire Statesman*, at 98.

On the Catholic doctrine of subsidiarity, see Hornsby-Smith, *An Introduction to Catholic Social Thought*, at 105-106, 187, 190, 226, 325, and 327.

AL SMITH: THE CATHOLIC AS PROGRESSIVE

On the flawed legacy of Progressivism, see Mannino, *Shaping America*, at 143-147, and Michael McGerr, *A Fierce Discontent: The Rise and Fall of the Progressive Movement in America 1870-1920* (New York: Free Press, 2003). McGerr covers the Progressive support of segregation of African-Americans at 182-202.

CHAPTER 7 – MICHAEL HARRINGTON: THE CATHOLIC AS SOCIALIST

The quotations from *The Catholic Catechism* which head this Chapter appear in paragraphs 1947 and 2448.

The best biography is Maurice Isserman, *The Other American: The Life of Michael Harrington* (New York: PublicAffairs, 2000) (paperback ed.). For a short biography, see 10 *American National Biography*, at 152-154.

Pete Hamill's quoting of Peter O'Toole's comment about "retired Catholics" appears in Hamill's article, "Confessions of a 'Retired' Catholic," in *Catholics in New York: Society, Culture, and Politics 1808 - 1946* (New York: Fordham University Press/Museum of the City of New York, 2008), 24.

EARLY WRITING, SOCIAL WORK, AND POLITICAL INVOLVEMENT

Harrington's time at the Catholic Worker is covered in Isserman,

The Other American, at 68-104, on which this account is largely based.

On Catholic Workers' desire to be saints, see the 1988 quotation attributed to Harrington in Isserman, *The Other American*, at 68.

The "as far Left" quotation appearing in the text referring to the Catholic Worker appears in Isserman, *The Other American*, at 70.

Harrington's Politics

Harrington's linkage of his conversion to socialism to his year at Yale Law School is recounted in Isserman, *The Other American*, at 48.

For Cogley's appearance before HUAC, and his questioning on Harrington, see Isserman, *The Other American*, at 152-155.

Harrington's description of the Democratic Socialist Organizing Committee as "democratic, humanist, and antiwar" appears in Isserman, *The Other American*, at 312.

Harrington's Pascalian wager regarding socialism and his view that "Socialism is still beginning..." are reported in Isserman, *The Other American*, at 311.

The Other America

The Other America: Poverty in the United States is available in multiple printings. I have used the Touchstone paperback edition, first published by Simon & Schuster in 1997. That edition also contains two subsequent essays, designated as "Afterwords," which were written by Harrington, covering "Poverty in the Seventies," and "Poverty and the Eighties." Where I have provided quotations from the book, the page numbers are included in parentheticals immediately following the sentence in which the quotation appears in the text.

Harrington's Political Philosophy

The quotation in the text from Harrington's article in the *New York Herald Tribune* regarding "the fate of Appalachia" appears in Isserman, *The Other American*, at 257.

The quotation in the text regarding Harrington's support of Walter Mondale's candidacy in 1984 because it united "all of the class and social forces we had deemed essential" appears in Isserman, *The Other American*, at 355.

Edward F. Mannino

HARRINGTON'S RELIGIOUS JOURNEY

Harrington's Salutatory Address at the Holy Cross graduation is covered and quoted in Isserman, *The Other American*, at 38.

Harrington's references to the "Jesuit house of cards" and to his "indecisive apostasy" are quoted in Isserman, *The Other American*, at 52.

Harrington's conclusion that he "no longer believed in the [Catholic] faith" is recounted in Isserman, *The Other American*, at 103-104.

For Harrington's reliance on Catholic just war theory and his admiration for Pope John XXIII, see Isserman, *The Other American*, at 137 and 172, 206.

The Acknowledgement to Dorothy Day and the Catholic Worker appears on page v. of Harrington, *The Other America*.

CHAPTER 8 – ROBERT F. KENNEDY: THE CATHOLIC AS PEOPLES' TRIBUNE

The quotation from Anna Quindlen which heads this chapter appears in *RFK: Collected Speeches*, eds. Edwin O. Guthman and C. Richard Allen (New York; Viking, 1993), xxix-xxx.

Out of the vast body of literature on Robert Kennedy, I found the following books the most helpful, in the order listed here: *Collected Speeches*; Edward R. Schmitt, *President of the Other America: Robert Kennedy and the Politics of Poverty* (Amherst, MA: University of Massachusetts Press, 2010); Thurston Clarke, *The Last Campaign: Robert F. Kennedy and 82 Days That Inspired America* (New York: Henry Holt and Company, 2008) ; Evan Thomas, *Robert Kennedy: His Life* (New York: Simon & Schuster, 2000); Konstantin Sidorenko, *Robert F. Kennedy: A Spiritual Biography* (New York: Crossroad Publishing Co., 2000); Jack Newfield, *Robert Kennedy: A Memoir* (New York: E.P. Dutton & Co., Inc., 1969) ; and Arthur M. Schlesinger, Jr., *Robert Kennedy and His Times* (Boston: Houghton Mifflin Company, 1978). Notably, the earlier books on Robert Kennedy devote little space to the influence of his Catholic faith on his policies. Schlesinger, for example, in 916 pages of text, lists only seven references to Kennedy's "religious faith" at page 1045 of his Index.

A Funeral Train

For descriptions and pictures of the crowds along the tracks of Robert Kennedy's funeral train, see Clarke, at 6, and "Robert Kennedy's Funeral Train," *Double Take*, Vol. 7, No. 4, Fall 2001, cover and 26.

Paul Fusco's pictures referenced in the text are reproduced in *Double Take*.

The quotation from the nurse about Robert Kennedy which is referenced in the text appears in *Double Take*, at 27.

Schlesinger's "Tribune of the Underclass" reference appears in Schlesinger, at 778.

The quotation from Robert Lowell which is referenced in the text appears in "Robert Kennedy: 1925-1968," in Robert Lowell, *Notebook 1967-68* (New York: Farrar, Straus and Giroux, 1969), 118.

The voting figures from the 1968 Democratic California presidential primary appear in Schmitt, at 218.

Robert Kennedy's Political Career

A helpful chronology of Robert Kennedy's life, including his political career, appears in Sidorenko, at 174-179.

Robert Kennedy's views about joining the McCarthy committee and his concession that "I was wrong," appear in Sidorenko, at 35.

Jack Newfield's "soldier, priest, radical, and football coach" description of Kennedy quoted in the text appears in Newfield, at 17.

Robert Kennedy's Religion

For Kennedy's experiences at St. Paul's and Portsmouth Priory, see Newfield, at 44; Thomas, at 32; and Sidorenko, at 99. The quotation in the text from Joseph Kennedy about Robert spending too much time on religious subjects appears in Sidorenko, at 99.

The Baltimore Catechism teachings on the Second Commandment appear in *Father McGuire's The New Baltimore Catechism and Mass, No.2*, (New York: Benziger Brothers, Inc., 1941) (official revised edition), 89-90.

Kennedy's practicing of his Catholic faith, including his Mass attendance, going to confession, serving as an altar boy, praying, saying the rosary, and reading the Bible to his children is covered in Newfield, at 44; Thomas, at 19 and 186; and Sidorenko, at 97 and 101.

The quotation in the text regarding Kennedy's recognition that "God's been good to me" appears in Clarke, at 104.

Kennedy's criticism of the Catholic Church as too conservative is recounted in Sidorenko, at 106.

Kennedy's "the hell with them" comment about college students not interested in hearing about hunger appears in Schmitt, at 1.

Kennedy's turn to Greek tragedy and Albert Camus after his brother's assassination is covered in Thomas, at 286-287, 319-321, 342, 345, 368, and 371; Sidorenko, at 108-109; and Newfield, at 58-59.

ROBERT KENNEDY'S POLICIES

The quotation in the text regarding the "Catholic ideals" in Robert Kennedy's "politics of poverty" appears in Schmitt, at 75. See also id. at 6, 16-17.

The quotation in the text from Kennedy's remarks in Gary, Indiana, about violence and human dignity appears in Clarke, at 151.

The quotation in the text from Kennedy regarding a spiritual deficiency in the American people appears in *Collected Speeches*, at 329.

The quotation in the text from Kennedy regarding decency being at the heart of his campaign appears in Clarke, at 56.

THE VIETNAM WAR

The quotation in the text from Kennedy's speech against the Vietnam War on the floor of the Senate appears in Sidorenko, at 167.

The quotation in the text from Kennedy's speech at Kansas State University questioning the morality of the Vietnam War appears in *Collected Speeches*, at 326.

The quotation in the text from Kennedy's Sacramento speech about the promise of the soldiers who die in Vietnam appears in Clarke, at 57.

The quotation in the text from Kennedy's speech to the University of Indiana medical students about black people carrying the burden of fighting the Vietnam War appears in *Collected Speeches*, at 342-343.

The quotation in the text from Kennedy's speech to the University of Indiana regarding spending billions in the name of the freedom of others appears in *Collected Speeches,* at 378.

POVERTY

Kennedy's Senate field trip to the Mississippi Delta is covered in Schmitt, at 177-179.

The quotation in the text from Cesar Chavez about Kennedy seeing things through the eyes of the poor appears in Clarke, at 79.

The quotation in the text from Kennedy's speech to the Americans for Democratic Action regarding welfare appears in Schmitt, at 124.

The quotation in the text with Kennedy's reference to welfare recipients being forced to rely on their fellow citizens to write them checks appears in *Collected Speeches,* at 385.

For Kennedy's policies to enlist private enterprise in the fight against poverty, see Schmitt, at 187-188, and *Collected Speeches,* at 389, 394. For his call for government to be the employer of last resort, see *Collected Speeches,* at 353, 393-394.

The quotation in the text from Kennedy's University of Alabama speech regarding jobs and homes appears in *Collected Speeches,* at 335.

RACISM

Kennedy's closeness to Native Americans and scheduling of campaign events in Native American venues is referenced in Clarke, at 155.

The quotation in the text from Kennedy's March 1968 Kansas speech on the poverty of Native Americans appears in *Collected Speeches*, at 328.

Kennedy's comparison of Wounded Knee to Dachau appears in Schmitt, at 204.

The quotation in the text from Kennedy's speech to The Friendly Sons of St. Patrick appears in *Collected Speeches*, at 108.

The quotation in the text from Kennedy's March 1968 speech to migrant farm workers appears in *Collected Speeches,* at 206.

EMPOWERMENT

Kennedy's new federalism is discussed in Schmitt, at 73-75 and 101-102.

The quotation in the text from Kennedy's April 1968 Nebraska speech on the need for small groups to plan their own future appears in *Collected Speeches,* at 373.

The quotation in the text regarding Kennedy's call for Washington to return decision-making power to local communities appears in *Collected Speeches,* at 389.

The quotation in the text regarding Kennedy's belief that the real answer to poverty lay with fully involving the private enterprise system appears in *Collected Speeches,* at 389. See also the discussion in Schmitt, at 125-126 and 275, n.36.

For a discussion of Kennedy's Bedford-Stuyvesant Project, see Schmitt, at 146-168. The quotation in the text from Kennedy regarding combining the best of community action with the best of private enterprise appears in *Collected Speeches,* at 189.

For a discussion of Kennedy's approach and the Catholic doctrine of subsidiarity, see Schmitt, at 74-75.

CATHOLIC TRIBUNE OF THE PEOPLE

The quotation from Aeschylus used by Robert Kennedy in his Indianapolis speech appears in *Collected Speeches,* at 357.

The quotations in the text about heroes appear in Miguel de Unamuno, *Tragic Sense of Life* (New York: Dover Publications, Inc., 1954) (paperback ed.), 128, 130.

PART III

CHAPTER 9 – CATHOLIC JUDGES AND HUMAN DIGNITY

The quotation from *The Catholic Catechism* which heads this Chapter appears in paragraphs 1929 and 1930. The quotation from Thomas Merton appears in *Conjectures of a Guilty Bystander*, at 219.

WILLIAM GASTON AND THE RIGHTS OF SLAVES

For an excellent general history of the changing positions of the Roman Catholic Church on slavery, see John T. Noonan, Jr., *A Church That Can and Cannot Change* (Notre Dame, IN: University of Notre Dame Press, 2005), 17-123. The quotation in the text from Bishop Kendrick on slavery is reprinted in *Creative Fidelity: American Catholic Intellectual Traditions*, eds. F. Scott Appleby, Patricia Byrne, and William L. Porter (Maryknoll, NY: Orbis Books, 2004), 167, 169-170.

The *Dred Scott* decision and Chief Justice Taney are discussed in Mannino, *Shaping America,* at 31-34. For an overview of southern laws on the treatment of slaves, see Kermit L. Hall, *The Magic Mirror* (New York: Oxford University Press, 1989), 131-134.

A short biography of William Gaston is found in 8 *American National Biography*, at 783-784. The best book-length biography is J. Herman Schauinger, *William Gaston: Carolinian* (Milwaukee, WI: Bruce Publishing Co., 1949). Gaston's remarks in favor of black suffrage are quoted in Schauinger, *William Gaston,* at 184.

Bishop England's 1829 estimate of twenty five Catholics in North Carolina is reported in James T. Fisher, *Communion of Immigrants: A History of Catholics in America* (New York: Oxford University Press, 2002) (paperback ed.), 39.

State v. Will is officially reported at 15 N.C. 121 (1834). The quotations from *State v. Will* in the text are reprinted in Schauinger, *William Gaston,* at 168-169. *State v. Manuel* is officially reported at 20 N.C. 385 (1838).

The reference to Gaston's "deeply religious" views is found in Thomas D. Morris, *Southern Slavery and the Law: 1619-1860* (Chapel Hill, NC: University of North Carolina Press, 1999), 459, n. 108

PIERCE BUTLER AND THE RIGHTS OF THE ACCUSED AND IMPAIRED

An excellent and balanced recent examination of Pierce Butler's legal career and Supreme Court opinions is presented in David R. Stras, "Pierce Butler: A Supreme Technician," 62 *Vanderbilt Law Review* 695 (2009). For brief biographies of Butler, see 4 *American National Biography*, at 105-107, and *The Oxford Companion to the Supreme Court of the United States*, 2d ed., editor in chief Kermit L. Hall (New York: Oxford University Press, 2005), 130-131. For a muckraking attack on Butler and his colleagues written during the New Deal, see Drew Pearson and Robert S. Allen, *The Nine Old Men* (Garden City, NY: Doubleday, Doran & Co., Inc., 1936), 116-138.

For Butler's alleged title, "Papal Delegate to the Supreme Court," see Pearson and Allen, *Nine Old Men*, at 116.

The "Abhorrence...of persistent and menacing crime" quotation in the text is reported in *Oxford Supreme Court*, at 131.

Olmstead v. United States is officially reported at 277 U.S. 438 (1928). The quotations from Justice Butler's dissenting opinion in that case appear at 277 U.S. 487-488. The quotation from Chief Justice Hughes is reported in Stras, *Pierce Butler*.

Buck v. Bell is officially reported at 274 U.S. 200 (1927). The case and its historical setting, as well as the contemporary debate at that time over eugenics, is analyzed in Mannino, *Shaping America*, at 143-145.

The alleged quotation from Justice Holmes on how "the Church beats the law" for Butler appears in Pearson and Allen, *Nine Old Men*, at 117. Nourse, *Reckless Hands,* at 30, suggests, without explicitly stating so, that Butler's vote was linked to his Catholic faith.

Skinner v. Oklahoma is officially reported at 316 U.S. 535 (1942). For an excellent review of both the historical background and the proceedings in that case, see Nourse, *Reckless Hands*.

FRANK MURPHY AND THE INTERNMENT OF JAPANESE AMERICANS

A good, one-volume biography of Frank Murphy is J. Woodford Howard, *Mr. Justice Murphy: A Political Biography* (Princeton, NJ: Princeton University Press, 1968). For brief biographies of Murphy, see 16 *American National Biography*, at 128-130, and *Oxford Supreme Court*, at 659-660.

The "reason and Christianity..." quotation is reported in Howard, *Justice Murphy*, at 175.

The Harvard official reference to the Trinity is reported in 16 *American National Biography*, at 130.

The quotations regarding "the Great Pulpit," and law as "a positive instrument for human betterment," are reported in Howard, *Justice Murphy*, at 228, 232.

The list of "F.M.'s Clients" appears on the inside back cover of Howard, *Justice Murphy*.

The "tempering justice with Murphy" quotation is reported in 16

American National Biography, at 129, which states that the quotation "may have" originated with Frankfurter.

Hirabayashi v. United States is officially reported at 320 U.S. 81 (1943). The quotations from Justice Murphy's concurring opinion appear at 320 U.S. 110, 111.

Korematsu v. United States is officially reported at 323 U.S. 214 (1944). The quotations from Justice Murphy's dissenting opinion appear at 323 U.S. 233, 234-235. The Catholic Church's concept of excommunication is explained in *The HarperCollins Encyclopedia of Catholicism*, general editor Richard P. McBrien (New York: HarperCollins Publishers, 1995), 500-501.

The background and history of the *Japanese Internment Cases* are explored in Mannino, *Shaping America*, at 129-135.

WILLIAM BRENNAN AND THE DEATH PENALTY

For biographies of William Brennan, see Seth Stern and Stephen Wermiel, *Justice Brennan: Liberal Champion* (New York: Houghton Mifflin Harcourt, 2010), and Kim Isaac Eisler, *A Justice for All: William J. Brennan, Jr., and the Decisions That Transformed America* (New York, Simon & Schuster 1993). For a brief biography of Brennan, see *Oxford Supreme Court*, at 102-105.

The Supreme Court confirmation hearing question about Brennan's religion and his response are reported in Stern and Wermiel, *Liberal Champion*, at 117-119, and in Eisler, *Justice for All*, at 118-119.

For Brennan's role in *Roe v. Wade*, see Stern and Wermiel, *Liberal Champion*, at 370-375, and Eisler, *Justice for All*, at 221-233.

Craig v. Boren is officially reported at 429 U.S. 190 (1976).

Brennan's view of the Constitution as embodying a vision of the supremacy of human dignity appears in a 1986 *South Texas Law Review* article he wrote, and is reported in *Oxford Supreme Court*, 104.

The evolution of Justice Brennan's view of the death penalty is covered in Chapter 17 of Stern and Wermiel, *Liberal Champion*, at 409-430, in a chapter entitled "Death & Dignity."

For a discussion of Brennan's use of the concept of human dignity, particularly in the death penalty cases, see Stern and Wermiel, *Liberal Champion*, at 166, and 418-423, the latter of which citation notes the use of the concept by Pope Leo XIII in the 1891 labor encyclical *Rerum Novarum* and by Monsignor John A. Ryan in his 1906 book *A Living Wage*. The authors nevertheless downplay any Catholic influence in Brennan's use of human dignity in his opinions, contending that Brennan's use of the concept "aligned" with the Catholic Church's call for a "consistent ethic of life," but adding that "Brennan invoked human dignity to condemn the death penalty earlier than any prominent figures within the Church." Id. at 422.

Furman v. Georgia is officially reported at 408 U.S. 238 (1972). The quotations from Justice Brennan's concurring opinion appear at 408 U.S. 270, 272-273.

The 1999 homily of Pope John Paul II quoted in the text is reported at United States Conference of Catholic Bishops, "Statements by the Holy Father on the Death Penalty," http://www.usccb.org (accessed June 30, 2006) under "Social Development and World Peace."

ANTHONY KENNEDY: ABORTION, CRIMINAL PUNISHMENT, GAY RIGHTS, AND HUMAN DIGNITY

For the "Papal Court" characterization, see Lexington, "The Papal Court," *The Economist,* January 28, 2005, 52.

The cartoon with the bishops' mitres appeared in the *Philadelphia Inquirer*. It was reprinted in Rick Garnett, "A chill wind from Rome...," http://prawfslawg.blogs.com (accessed April 20, 2007), which also discusses the bloggers' comments on religion as a basis for the partial birth abortion decision in *Gonzales v. Carhart*.

For a brief biography of Anthony Kennedy, see *Oxford Supreme Court,* at 555-557. Frank J. Colucci, *Justice Kennedy's Jurisprudence: The Full and Necessary Meaning of Liberty* (Lawrence, KS: University Press of Kansas, 2009) provides a valuable overview of Justice Kennedy's legal philosophy, which Colucci finds rooted in an expansive view of "liberty," informed in part by Catholic concepts of human dignity. In developing Kennedy's jurisprudence, Colucci provides additional support for concluding, as I do, that Catholic judges often utilize Catholic teachings to support conclusions which they come to based upon their overall legal philosophy, and not upon their religion. Colucci is especially insightful in his linking of Justice Kennedy's use of a coercion test in Establishment Clause cases to the teachings of *Dignitatis Humanae* (16-20, 31-33). Less compelling are his treatments of *Lawrence v. Texas* (21-28, 33-35) and certain death penalty cases (28-31, 33). As I argue in the text, Kennedy's approaches in these cases are inconsistent with Catholic teachings on homosexual conduct and the death penalty.

Stenberg v. Carhart is officially reported at 530 U.S. 914 (2000). The quotations from Justice Kennedy's dissenting opinion appear at 530 U.S. 958-959, 961.

Gonzales v. Carhart is officially reported at 550 U.S. 124 (2007).

For a detailed analysis of the Supreme Court's abortion jurisprudence, see Mannino, *Shaping America*, at 230-250.

Kansas v. Marsh is officially reported at 548 U.S. 163 (2006).

Weems v. United States is officially reported at 217 U.S. 349 (1910).

Graham v. Florida is officially reported at 560 U.S. — (2010).

Roper v. Simmons is officially reported at 543 U.S. 551 (2005).

Kennedy v. Louisiana is officially reported at 554 U.S. 407 (2008).

Brown v. Plata is officially reported at 563 U.S. — (2011).

Barber v. Thomas is officially reported at 560 U.S. — (2010).

Lawrence v. Texas is officially reported at 539 U.S. 558 (2003). The quotations from Justice Kennedy's majority opinion appear at 539 U.S. 567 and 575.

CATHOLIC JUDGES AND HUMAN DIGNITY

For my previous discussion of the influence of the dominant political culture of the times upon the decision-making process of Supreme Court Justices, see Mannino, *Shaping America*, at 3-6, 273-275.

The quotation from Father Neuhaus on human dignity and autonomy is from Richard John Neuhaus, *American Babylon: Notes of a Christian Exile* (New York: Basic Books, 2009), at 191.

PART IV

CHAPTER 10- SISTERS OF COMPASSION: HOW AMERICAN NUNS HELP THE HELPLESS

NUNS IN AMERICAN SOCIETY

For histories of Catholic Sisters in America, see Carol K. Coburn and Martha Smith, *Spirited Lives: How Nuns Shaped Catholic Culture and American Life, 1826-1920* (Chapel Hill, NC: University of North Carolina Press, 1999), and John J. Fialka, *Sisters: Catholic Nuns and the Making of America* (New York: St. Martin's Griffin, 2003).

On nuns serving as nurses in the Civil War, see George C. Rable, *God's Almost Chosen Peoples: A Religious History of the American Civil War* (Chapel Hill, NC: University of North Carolina Press, 2010), 210-213; Fialka, *Sisters*, at 5-6, 58-70; Coburn and Smith, *Spirited Lives*, at 63. The quotation in the text from the Maine soldier appears in Rable, *God's Almost Chosen Peoples*, at 212.

For the contributions of nuns to the settling of the American West, see Fialka, *Sisters*, at 92-105.

For the service of nuns to Native Americans, see Coburn and Smith, *Spirited Lives*, at 105-118.

The 2010 statistics on American nuns' education and racial and ethnic backgrounds are taken from "State of the Sisters," *America*, February 14, 2010, at 8.

For the number of nuns in the United States in 1968 and 2003, respectively, see Fialka, *Sisters*, at 15, 17.

For the 2009/2011 statistics on the number and ages of American nuns, and the statistics on the rapidly declining number of Catholic hospitals led by nuns and priests, see Kevin Sack, "Nuns, a 'Dying Breed,' Fade From Leadership Roles at Catholic Hospitals," *New York Times*, August 20, 2011.

ELIZABETH SETON

For biographical background on Elizabeth Seton, see Elaine Murray Stone, *Elizabeth Bayley Seton: An American Saint* (New York: Paulist Press, 1993); Joseph I. Dirvin, *The Soul of Elizabeth*

Seton: A Spiritual Portrait (San Francisco: Ignatius Press, 1990) ; Benedict Groeschel, *I Am with You Always: A Study of the History and Meaning of Personal Devotion to Jesus Christ for Catholic, Orthodox, and Protestant Christians* (San Francisco: Ignatius Press, 2010), 425-430; *Catholic History Encyclopedia*, at 1277-1280.

The quotation in the text from Mother Seton's letter to the Filicchis appears in Dirvin, *Soul of Elizabeth Seaton*, at 158. Capital letters in the original letter have been removed.

ROSE HAWTHORNE

For biographical information on Rose Hawthorne, see Groeschel, *I Am with You* Always, at 549-554; Lou Ella Hickman, "Profiles in Greatness: Rose Hawthorne," *Spirituality for Today*, Vol. 15, No. 2, September, 2010; George Weigel, "The Remarkable Rose Hawthorne," *The Catholic Difference*, September 16, 2009.

The "fire...lighted in my heart" quotation in the text from Rose Hawthorne appears in Groeschel, *I Am with You Always*, at 550.

KATHERINE DREXEL

For biographical information on Katherine Drexel, see Consuela Marie Duffy, *Katherine Drexel: A Biography* (Bensalem, PA: Sisters of the Blessed Sacrament, 1966) (this book is particularly valuable for its extensive quotations from Drexel's letters and notebooks; its author was a member of Drexel's order); Mary van Balen Holt, *Meet Katherine Drexel: Heiress and God's Servant of the Oppressed* (Ann Arbor, MI: Servant Publications, 2002) ; *Catholic History Encyclopedia*, at 457-459; 6 *American National Biography*, at 916-917.

The formation of the 1871 Drexel and Company partnership with J. P. Morgan is described in Ron Chernow, *The House of Morgan* (New York: Atlantic Monthly Books, 1990), 33-35.

Katherine Drexel's chart of the pros and cons of her following a religious vocation is reprinted in Duffy, at 111-112 and in Holt, at 39.

For an account of opposition by white residents and black ministers to Drexel's acquisition of a property in Nashville, Tennessee in 1905 for use as a school for African-American girls, see Duffy, at 252-262.

Edward F. Mannino

For a list of the Indian and black missions assisted by Drexel, see Duffy, at 269-271.

MARY SCULLION

For biographical information on Mary Scullion, see Margaret Gordon Kender, "The Influential Sister Mary Scullion," *St. Anthony Messenger*, August 2010; Tom Roberts, "Time cites nun among 100 most influential," *National Catholic Reporter*, April 2, 2009; Fialka, *Sisters*, at 226-230, 295-300.

For information on Project H.O.M.E., see Project H.O.M.E. Annual Report 2009/2010, and www.projecthome.org.

The quotations in the text from Jon Sobrino and Mary Scullion regarding taking Jesus off the cross appear in Tom Roberts, "Time cites nun"

The quotations in the text from Project H.O.M.E.'s mission statement and vision appear in its 2009/2010 Annual Report, as does the quotation from Senator Casey.

CONCLUSION: THE CHANGING VIEW OF AMERICAN CATHOLICS

I am indebted to Bruce Kuklick for his suggestion to include the portrayal of Catholics in Hollywood movies to advance the themes in this Chapter.

I have benefitted greatly from two recent books by Catholic historians which discuss most of the movies mentioned in the text. These books are Christopher Shannon, *Bowery to Broadway: The American Irish in Classic Hollywood Cinema* (Scranton, PA: University of Scranton Press, 2010), and Anthony Burke Smith, *The Look of Catholics.*

CATHOLIC PRIESTS AS HEROES IN AMERICAN MOVIES: FROM FATHER FLANAGAN TO WAR HEROES TO LABOR PRIESTS

For insightful summaries and analyses of "Boys Town," "the Fighting 69th,"" "Going My Way," and "The Bells of St. Mary's," see Shannon, *Bowery to Broadway*, at 106-152, and Smith, *The Look of Catholics*, at 46-53, 56-59, and 66-87.

For the work of Father John Corridan, and the "Father Barry" speech in "On the Waterfront," see Morris, *American Catholic*, at 208-209.

BING CROSBY: THE CATHOLIC PRIEST AS REGULAR AMERICAN

For a short biography of Bing Crosby, see 5 *American National Biography*, at 773-775. The "border-crossing" nature of Father O'Malley is noted in Smith, *The Look of Catholics*, at 72.

THE DARKER SIDE

Snyder v. Phelps is officially reported at 562 U.S. — (2011).

The quotations in the text from Albert Camus appear in his novel, *The Plague* (New York: Modern Library, 1948), 278.

Index

H

I

J

K

L

Edward F. Mannino

Edward F. Mannino

ABOUT THE AUTHOR

Edward F. Mannino is a lawyer and historian, with high honors degrees in both History and Law from the University of Pennsylvania. The author of four previous books on Law and on American Legal History, he has taught at the University of Pennsylvania, Temple University Law School, and Chestnut Hill College. Mannino is a founding director of the Historical Society of the United States District Court for the Eastern District of Pennsylvania, and has served as a member of the Board of Overseers of the University of Pennsylvania School of Arts and Sciences, and as a Commonwealth Trustee of Temple University, having been appointed to that position by the Governor of Pennsylvania as his representative. He lives with his wife, Antoinette K. O'Connell, in Gwynedd Valley, Pennsylvania.